COME SEPTEMBER

Journey of a High School Teacher

A Memoir by John Bolinger

Dedicated to high school teachers across America and to the work they do, despite myriad obstacles on a daily basis, including going without recognition, and many eating corn dogs on a stick for lunch on Mondays and fish sticks on Fridays...for years on end.

Preface: Recounting how John met Bel Kaufman and how the book's title came about

Chapter 1 “Lunar Landing” John, as a new college graduate seeks a job, feeling amusingly sorry for himself along the way but finding at last what he believes will be his calling as a high school teacher in Indiana. He meets his first principal and begins the teaching journey.

Chapter 2 “Bonjour, Y'All.” Beginning of John's career introduces him to a few of the galaxy of entertaining characters, including another teacher of French, who will broaden his views...and other characters encountered, including the English Department chair, who has taught since the 1920's

Chapter 3 “Onward and Upward” Surviving that first day of classes after expecting a "blackboard jungle" experience

Chapter 4 “I Dunno” Freshman, Johnny Madison, provides first big teaching challenge and some frustration

Chapter 5 “When I Break Outta Here” Multiple teaching surprises including some karate and a temporary triumph for all

Chapter 6 “Free Condiments” A cafeteria brawl and how John breaks it up

Chapter 7 “The Sound of Bells” Some school day patterns become established, and eccentric characters are encountered in both students and faculty

Chapter 8 “Faculty Feuds and Some Freedom” Teacher rivalries and John's first apartment

Chapter 9 “Matters of Conscience” Attempts to help a wayward freshman before a battle with the principal over a Vietnam War student protest

Chapter 10 “Wonders Never Ceasing” Amorous adventures of seniors in the auditorium balcony

Chapter 11 “Freshmen Fake Book Reports and Other Foibles” Devious means to get students to turn in homework

Chapter 12 “Confessions of a Public School Teacher” Very individual way to vent teacher frustrations safely with no one being injured

Chapter 13 “Summer Respite” Some grad work in Paris, France with new characters and even a love interest

Chapter 14 “Back Home in Indiana” Some revelations about teaching in Northwest Indiana being different from teaching elsewhere

Chapter 15 “Rivalries, Cars, and Hungarians” Conflicts between faculty members, John's first car, and a new student from abroad and how he fits in

COME SEPTEMBER
The Journey of a High School Teacher

PREFACE

The fall of 1969 I met Bel Kaufman, author of UP THE DOWN STAIRCASE (released in 1964 and later made into a film starring Sandy Dennis). Ms. Kaufman was the feature speaker at the Hammond Civic Center that year for Teachers' Institute, the two-day series of meetings and workshops attended by all public school teachers in Hammond, Indiana in late October in those years. As someone who admired her, I wanted very much to speak with her, even if briefly. By winding my way after the program through two security guards and crowds of other school teachers, I came upon the stalwart lady, whose hair was swept back on one side as though she had just come inside after an encounter with a strong wind. She was wearing a smart tweed suit and a sumptuously patterned silk scarf.

She looked at me as I approached her before the next person could accost her. Ms. Kaufman was even more gracious and charming than I had hoped, and what I remember still from our brief exchange of words is her telling me that as a first-year teacher I had ahead of me a journey filled with more wondrous things than I could at that time imagine. She was right. No one, despite his having completed practice teaching for his B.A., could have conjured up images of the cast of eccentric characters to be encountered, those awful faculty meetings, open house for parents, PTA meetings, cafeteria duty, club sponsoring, planning lessons, grading mountains of homework papers and tests, or even standing before that first group of staring freshmen in my own classroom.

Looking back, I can see now that for the first couple of years I was a pretty terrible teacher, dependent upon soul-shrinking teachers' manuals, standardized tests, and the empty conviction that one size fits all. Methods classes I had taken in college proved of little use in what gradually revealed itself to be the "real world" of public education, which over time would become my world, the center of my life, and the corps of my identity for thirty-five years, years upon which I look back with affection and with a sincere hope that now in a time of turmoil and financial stress, public education in America will find its way again through the dedication of other teachers, parents, and students themselves. I want this book to reflect the love and respect I have for the teaching profession, but I want also to show the light side of the years I spent instructing kids in English and French classes and helping them to discover who they were and of what they were capable.

One confession I must share with the reader is that COME SEPTEMBER was not my first choice for a title. The first one came from an experience I had teaching English in summer school during the 1980's, when one morning during ten o'clock break, I stood in the hallway outside my classroom to help maintain a sense of order while students congregated around locker bay C. Unintentionally, I found myself eavesdropping on a conversation between Eric, one of my students, and another kid whose voice I didn't recognize. The sentences I heard Eric speak, which will remain forever in my memory, were, "No, man, you don't understand. Skeletons ain't got no tits." The two boys were obviously unaware that I was listening, and I was so stunned by Eric's words, that I was immobilized until the bell rang for classes to resume. I never asked him about what I had heard him say to his buddy. During the years that have elapsed since that summer morning, I have regretted over and over again not

asking Eric what the hell he was talking about. Now, I suppose it will remain one of those mysteries that stays on one of the back shelves of my mind, with my question forever unanswered, unless Eric reads this book and manages to contact me so that I may some day go peacefully to my grave through the simple resolution of what he meant that day. More than one of my friends has told me that SKELETONS AIN'T GOT NO TITS may get people's attention but may not necessarily sell books. I have, therefore, opted for the more docile title of COME SEPTEMBER, even though the book promises to share many equally irreverent anecdotes about my years in the classroom.

Bel Kaufman celebrated her 100th birthday in May of 2011. This is just another reason for me to feel inspired by someone who taught high school and survived. It gives me the hope that I may celebrate my 100th too, only my celebration will not occur until March of 2046.

John Bolinger

Chapter 1 Lunar Landing

Final exams had been taken and graded on June 8, and stacks of them were scattered on my desk as well as on a conference table next to it. It was June 9, 2004. Students were all gone by then, preparing to celebrate another summer, free of the constraints of homework, pop quizzes, and the watchful eyes of the teachers who were now sitting over cups of coffee at desks covered with scan sheets and pens nearly bled dry of their red ink. Rows of empty student desks stared back at me, and voices and faces of students I had taught in that room for so many years began to crowd my mind with recollections. It was all coming to an end, because the next day I would be officially retired, and the journey of teaching that Bel Kaufman had told me about years before would be over in just a matter of hours. At times like that, reflection has a way of forcing its way into one's mind to open reservoirs of memory that make us put things into some sort of perspective. I was remembering that hot July afternoon of 1969, and those first steps of that journey.

I had just graduated from Ball State University in Muncie, Indiana with a B.A. that would, if I could find a job, allow me to teach high school English and French. In June I had traveled by bus to Leonardtown, Maryland and to Lexington, Massachusetts for job interviews for teaching high school in one of those cities. Both places were urban disasters, still using text books from the 1950's, overcrowded, and using eastern accents that would have taken me a long time to get used to. As a recent and still unemployed college graduate, I was without money or a car, managing to get back to Hammond, Indiana by bus from Washington, D.C., spending literally my last dollar, and seated all the way on that bus next to an elderly woman with long, bright red, curving, talon-like fingernails, and hair a flaming color that has, I'm fairly certain, never been found in nature. During the entire trip she was reading Truman Capote's IN COLD BLOOD, turning to me every few minutes to comment on the grislier aspects of the book, usually when I was taking a bite of one of the Three Muskateers candy bars I had purchased with my last seventy-five cents in DC to keep myself alive for the trip home.

Arriving back at my parents' house, I was hungry, exhausted, poor, and as unsure of my future as Benjamin from my then favorite film, THE GRADUATE, ever was. After eating an egg salad sandwich, I went straight to my room to ponder my next move. My desk was buried in college text books from the previous four years that, had I been able to sell them for what we had originally paid, would have kept me financially independent for years. Remembering all the money Mom and Dad had shelled out for them, I wondered too if the books would ever prove to be of any use. My graduation tassel hanging from the closet door knob served only to remind me of the rather grand show college had been and made me wonder again what it was all for. Visions of selling apples on street corners played themselves in my brain as I imagined my plight to be like that of any of a host of oppressed literary characters, including The Little Match Girl. It was almost funny.

Then my mother knocked on my bedroom door, opening it just enough to poke her head inside with a sympathetic smile. I asked her in, and she sat on the twin bed that had been my brother David's before he joined the army and went off to Viet Nam. After a minute she asked simply, “So what are your plans?”

"I wish I had a plan," I answered. "I signed no contract out East. Should I make a hobo stick and begin looking for a good box car down at the stock yards?"

She gave me one of those looks of half disapproval and half recognition of my comment's humorous intent. Then she hit me with an obvious solution to my sad state.

"Have you thought about teaching here in Hammond?"

That question stopped me in my tracks for two reasons, one that my status as a college senior and all the swagger that went with it was suddenly shattered by a harsh look at reality, the kind I had encountered when I found out there was really no Santa Claus. Second, it ended any romantic notions on my part of venturing away from my home town to become the Mr. Chips of some school out East. I felt like George Bailey standing in the front yard of his parents' home listening to that train whistle in the distance and knowing he was going nowhere. Mom was well aware of the effect her blunt question was having on me, so she simply looked down, waiting for some kind of response. In a way, I suppose her directness was way more efficient than trying to ease slowly through a list of fake options that we would both have recognized as silly.

Without saying a word, I got up and went downstairs to phone the School City of Hammond to make an appointment with William McNabney, who was in charge of the school city's personnel. I was told by his secretary to bring my college transcripts.

The bus ride to downtown Hammond gave me a few more minutes to reflect on the fact that some of my peers from high school were off to Europe for grad school, while others were going into the Peace Corps to serve in exotic locations like Africa and India. And there I was staying in my home town, perhaps to become ossified by holding on tightly to a grubby little salary in a nontenured position for at least five years in one of four high schools.

I braced myself for the coming interview, telling myself that I needed to show some enthusiasm and energy when talking with Mr. McNabney, and that it would be an actual job, one that would at least pay my bills until I could find something more "appropriate," which meant a place where I could wear my Scottish tweed jacket with the suede elbow patches. I look back now at my snobbery and find it laughable. I wanted and expected respect and even admiration, just for having that lowly B.A. but had no idea how much difficult and unappreciated work lay ahead or how long and arduous a struggle it would take to bring a sense of real purpose, satisfaction, and pride in what I would be doing. At the time, however, I believed that somehow that B.A. was enough to make me omniscient and dazzling to the teenagers, who would populate my classes daily. I believed too that my tweed jacket, silk necktie, and fashionable gold-wired eyeglasses would take care of the rest. Oh, the innocence of freshly minted college graduates!

The board of education building for Hammond at that time was a classical stone structure on Hohman Avenue. It had once been a bank during the 1920's and 1930's but retained an immense dignity in its graceful stone steps and Ionic columns flanking the two very tall entrance doors of oak and polished brass. At the reception desk I was told to be seated on a carved mahogany bench that looked and felt like a church pew. The receptionist wore her hair in a tight bun and had on incongruously elaborate cat's eye glasses with a chain that moved in little waves with each motion of her head. There was also a pencil stabbed into that bun of hair, as though some tiny hunter had just speared it. On her fingers were rubber filing caps, and between her lips a couple of paper clips, which seemed to have little effect on her speaking to tell me that Mr. McNabney was ready to see me.

His name was on a brass plaque over his door on the second floor, where there were other rooms for finance, city school attendance records, and the superintendent's office. I knocked, and Mr. McNabney asked me to come in. He was a tall, stately man with an angular jaw and high cheek bones. His receding hair line only added to his impressive appearance. His demeanor was softened by a friendly smile and eyeglasses worn near the end of his nose. Standing up but remaining behind his desk, he offered his hand and asked me to be seated in a chair facing him. He commented briefly on the heat of the afternoon, adding that he hoped it would rain to help cool things off a bit. To this day I remember and admire him for the way he put me at ease while questioning me on my views about teaching and my principal goals for working in a classroom. I felt myself babbling and cannot tell you what I said, but he seemed to like whatever I was explaining, and he also liked my transcripts, overlooking perhaps the "D" I received in my P.E. classes of swimming and tennis. He also read the gracious comments written by a few of my profs and nodded in a way that made him look pleased. Finally, he looked up and asked if I would choose Gavit High School, my alma mater, or Morton High (named after the 19th Century governor, Oliver P. Morton). Though MHS was farther from my parents' house, I chose it just because one of my cousins had graduated as valedictorian in 1968.

Mr. M made a quick phone call to Mr. Perkins, the principal of Morton High School. "Yes, Walter, I'll send him right over," he said while smiling at me and winking. He gave me back my transcripts after his secretary had made photo copies and then wished me luck in my interview with Mr. Perkins.

Riding the bus to Hessville, where Morton High School was, gave me half an hour to consider again where my life might be going, perhaps a journey in the proverbial hand basket for all I knew. The bus route at that time did not include stops on Grand Avenue, where the school was, so I had to walk a couple of blocks, which included an open field filled with stickers that managed to find homes all over my cotton summer slacks. When the building came into view, I was shocked to see a sprawling blond brick edifice that looked more like some kind of factory or other industrial creation. The older Morton had been built by the WPA in 1940 and had been called affectionately "The Governor's Mansion" by its students. This newer building, however, had been constructed in 1967, when featureless, gulag architecture was reaching its zenith of dullness. The new school was really a complex of connected buildings that ended on the south side at a huge auditorium.

I entered the north office complex through the big red doors I would be using for the next thirty-five years. Walking down a wheelchair ramp toward the main office, I was startled by a view to my right of a very long hallway that seemed to go on forever, tapering to a distant vanishing point, like something in a Surrealist painting by Salvador Dali. Only a few open doors broke the sterile, seemingly unending lines of that view.

Another door led me into the main office, where there was a long counter almost the length of the whole room, separating a waiting area of chairs and a wall of faculty mail boxes from the area where secretaries had their desks outside yet another room, which was the principal's office, where the head secretary, Mrs. Kovacek, led me and knocked on the door.

Unlike Mr. McNabney, Mr. Perkins neither stood nor offered his hand, but remained seated behind his grand fortress of a desk. The room's character was like that of the building's exterior, minimally decorated, and rather cold, leading me to suppose that I need not expect the least bit of cheer, sympathy, or warmth. Indeed, the man behind the desk fulfilled my earlier view of the building's nature by inviting me to sit in the chair before his desk, while he held both hands in front of him, fingers and thumbs curving inward and touching to form what looked strangely like an empty little bird's cage.

He examined me with his eyes in a way that made me know he was already judging me and wanted me to realize his power and authority. My next thought was that he must be a man of very low self-confidence, someone perhaps who hid, not only behind a massive desk, but also behind a demeanor of complete indifference. I thought also that I should give him a chance to show that there might actually be a sensitive or even frightened being of terrible insecurity residing beneath that imperious facade.

He asked me about my interests and how I had enjoyed student teaching at Griffith High School the year before. When I replied that I considered the experience a success for me as well as for my students, I spoke in a matter-of-fact way, without enthusiasm, which I thought suited him. He then told me he would phone the department chairs of English and foreign language to arrange introductions and my scheduling of classes for first semester.

His saying these things made my heart thump faster, so that I was sure he would see it pounding right through my shirt. My eardrums began to pound as well so that for a while, I saw his lips moving but heard little of what he was saying. As he was looking at the ceiling anyway in a most disinterested manner, I took the opportunity of removing some of the field stickers from my slacks and dropping them into a nearby waste basket. The message that I was being engaged as a faculty member was not actually spoken, but in my brain it was flashing in neon lights with a brass band playing and my heartbeat providing the drums.

Mr. Perkins then called one of the secretaries to give me a tour of the building and to give me a key to room 248, even though I would have to see Mr. McNabney again to sign my contract, which for teaching four full classes a day, doing cafeteria lunch duty, and helping with the debate team, would pay precisely $6, 874.93. That seemed a princely sum to me at the time, even though after deductions for taxes and pension, I took home exactly $226 every two weeks, which in 2012 would hardly pay my grocery bill.

The tour of the building was long and a bit mind-numbing after seeing so many rooms that looked pretty much the same. Some were more memorable than others, like the auditorium, that seated 1500, which seemed enormous to me, even though assemblies had to be given twice to accommodate the school enrollment of 2300. The stage area was grand enough to handle even large productions like WEST SIDE STORY. There was also a small auditorium that was used for faculty and PTA meetings.

The library was filled with high quality wooden furniture, including very handsome card catalog cabinets. There were large pots of plants and interesting paintings and posters on all the walls. The space was filled with light from the south wall of windows that overlooked a charming courtyard garden. Seeing that room and meeting the cheerful and warm librarian, Mr. Fletcher, made me know I would be happy as a teacher there.

As it was late July, summer school was still in session, so there were students on break in the cafeteria, where television sets were tuned in to news coverage of the United States lunar landing on July 20. I became transfixed by the images and squeezed in between students sitting on a cafeteria bench. They hardly noticed me as we all watched intently those televised movies and photos of American astronauts walking on the surface of the moon and those celestial images of our planet seen like a big blue marble from out in space.

When I left that afternoon to go home, I knew that my life was on the verge of change, discovery, and adventure, not as an astronaut, but as the next best thing....a high school teacher.

Chapter 2 Bonjour, Y'All

Mrs. Charlotte Graham was a teacher of French and also chair of the Foreign Language Department in which Spanish and German were also offered. When I began teaching at Morton High School in the fall of 1969, Mrs. Graham was somewhere in her fifties. Petite and always fastidiously dressed in tweed skirts, silk blouses, and tight-fitting cashmere sweaters, she would begin each school day wearing high heels to accentuate her still lovely legs, but after homeroom, she would slip into the faculty lounge to change into her green leather sandals. The only stockings she ever wore were pure silk due to her allergies to synthetic fabrics. Her right eye was glass, and it was rumored that the reason she divided her classes, always with boys on the left, was that her rather coquettish behavior was more successful when the boys were all in plain view. Evidently, girls in her classes suffered from an appalling lack of attention, and a few of them came to realize that as long as they weren't even seen anyway, there was no need to attend class, except on test days.

When I met Charlotte Graham in August of that year, her flirtations with me were quite charming until it became apparent that, due to shrinking French class enrollment, she had no interest in or intention of relinquishing any of them to me, which would mean her having to teach an English class, something she considered far beneath her. She was sweetly apologetic about the fact that there were only four French classes, but it became quite clear that I would be teaching only English classes for a while, despite my offer to stand in the school hallways with a big French baguette and beat students into seeing their counselors to sign up for French classes. Mrs. Graham's only response to my attempt at humor was a weakly forced smile.

The faculty lounge/cafeteria, which in those days was usually filled with cigarette smoke that poured into the corridor with every opening of the door, was also segregated by sex. There was a social studies table at which that department of geography, government, and economics teachers were all men, almost all of them coaches of sports as well. Entering the area of that smoke-shrouded table as a woman was apparently verboten, though there were no written laws on the subject or signs to help some poor lady know that she would be shunned. None of this, however, stopped Charlotte Graham, who not only stood to chat with the men, but actually sat at the table with them, flirting outrageously with them in her temporarily exaggerated southern accent, as though she had never ventured north of the Mason/Dixon Line. The men at that table always called her "Miss Scarlet" in drawls with varying degrees of success. I always wondered how she might teach French pronunciation to her students and used to imagine each of her classes beginning with, "Bonjour, y'all" and then going "south" from there. In any event, my association with her would be minimal until there was a French class for me in order to make me a member of her department.

Just a few days before the start of school that year I met Miss Winifred Mason, the chair of Morton's English Department. A statuesque woman at five feet nine with a dignified hair style of tinted blue, she had been teaching since the 1920's, when municipal law had demanded that female school teachers not be seen alone in public after nine in the evening. Miss Mason would never have allowed anyone to address her as "Ms." She was of another era but wore timelessly tailored Chanel-like suits and carried herself with a noble posture that made her an automatic figure of authority that no student or even other faculty member would ever dare to challenge.

Despite her stately demeanor, Miss Mason would prove to be my greatest ally in the struggle to find my way through that first year of teaching. She would be retiring in the spring of 1970 after forty-four years of teaching, which still amazes me, considering that most teachers nowadays stay in the profession only five years, many of those people not even staying on a daily basis past three in the afternoon, beating the kids out to the parking lot. Miss Mason took me under her wing before making her exit from teaching.

As Labor Day approached, I grew more than a little nervous about the first day of school and the clientele I might be facing. I began to have nightmares about the 1955 movie, BLACKBOARD JUNGLE, starring Glenn Ford. In one dream I was holding a large notebook in front of me to fend off flying objects being hurled by students. The dream made scenes between Glenn Ford and his savage classes look like Miss Anna and the Siamese children singing, “Getting to Know You.” My imagination ran amok with visions of wild freshmen swinging from light fixtures, a puddle of Elmer’s Glue on the seat of my chair, and rubber bands used to shoot paper clips at me, like little harpoons. News headlines haunted me. “Teacher Carried Out of Classroom on Stretcher After Students Launch Unabridged Dictionary at His Head!”

Tuesday morning arrived finally, and I felt a bit the way I had felt going off to kindergarten years before in my Buster Brown shoes, reindeer cardigan, and crooked bow-tie. Though everything I had learned in college should have helped to prepare me for the world of teaching, all of my previous learning seemed to be a long series of blurred images and recollections that first morning. My old friend Bob Birchard, with whom I had graduated from high school, would also be teaching at MHS in the English Department and would be giving me a ride to and from school each day in his red MG convertible until I could buy my own car. I was at first alarmed by his seeming confidence and his already having a sports car. At that stage, my head and wallet felt as empty as Silas Marner’s address book.

All the teachers from all the Hammond schools were required to attend what would come to be called “mass meetings” at the Civic Center, the only place in town that could hold that many people. I believe the same pep-talk speech was used every year that I taught. Catch phrases like, “a new beginning” were used without fail or shame. “We must meet the new challenges of education” became yet another platitude to be repeated yearly in that huge, yawning space. My favorite was, “We are preparing our students for the future.” Of course, it was all still new to me that first time, and I listened intently, hoping for some brilliant statement that would help guide me through that first year in the classroom. The statement never came, probably because the main speaker was usually the superintendent of schools, and for all the years I taught, we never had a leader in that position, who was anything more than a money-grubbing business manager, devoid of any real interest in education itself or with any of the eloquence or sensitivity necessary to help inspire any of his underlings, who continued to grind their ways through school days across the city.

At any rate, there were no students in attendance the first day, which the teacher's association had set aside as much-needed organization time for teachers to prepare for the arrival of students for classes the next day. Since those days, grand-standing politicians have increased the number of school days to a required 183, as though the number of days in classrooms increases what is learned, when the quality of those days and what is taught should have been the focus. The public, though, can deal more easily with numbers, and the larger, the better. We are now learning gradually again that it is what happens in the days a student is in his classes, not the number of days he is there. That prep day for teachers meant a faculty meeting, department meetings, coordinating textbooks, writing lesson plans, and arranging individual classrooms with desks and bulletin boards. Department chairs would be giving out the semester's supplies of ditto masters, paper clips, rubber bands, red pens, typewriter ribbons, and aspirin. There were no computers or photo-copy machines. It was a time that to young teachers of today would seem an era of ancient cave drawings. In fact, if that world of education could be captured in cartoon form, it would seem to modern educators like watching THE FLINTSTONES, at least in terms of technology.

Certainly teaching has changed over the past forty-three years, because the world itself has changed. Attention spans are much shorter (Thank you, MTV and video games.), and diversity continues to increase in every classroom. Yet, behind the masks we all wear are the basic needs that have always existed, primarily the desire to succeed and to be accepted as a useful part of one's world. Technology has made its mark through computers and faster modes of communication (not necessarily the quality of communication), but in a recent, independent survey, high school students across the country were asked what they liked best about their schools. Virtually no one even mentioned computers, movie equipment, or any other forms of technology. Swimming pools and sports equipment were not mentioned either. In the responses, people were always the focus of what was meaningful. Even computers have not changed that.

My first faculty meeting in the small auditorium was that Tuesday morning after Labor Day. It was an experience that taught me in only forty minutes as much as I would ever learn about human nature and group dynamics.

There was a raised stage area with a podium at the center, where Mr. Perkins stood over a stack of notes. His glasses were down at the tip of his nose, a position he used in order to stare over the top of them at anyone he wanted to intimidate into paying more attention. He was the only one that day wearing a suit and necktie, which I suspected he saw as symbols of his power and authority. A minute after ten he was already glaring at the assemblage, some of whom showed their utter contempt at having to be there by doing crossword puzzles, reading newspapers, writing letters, doodling, and the chair of the math department already asleep, was snoring lightly in the back of the room.

I almost felt sorry for Mr. Perkins until I remembered my frigid reception in his office a month before. The most offensive member of the audience was Mr. Farrel of the Social Studies Department, who had brought with him several large rubber bands with which he proceeded to construct a cat's cradle, even after the meeting began. It would come to be extremely important over the years to identify the department in which one taught. When asked what one taught, it was as important as naming one's nationality. Stereotypes were easily formed for coaches as well as for prissy English teachers. That little galaxy was expected to revolve around the pompous and self-righteous Mr. Perkins, but many of the planets and satellites were dangerously out of orbit.

My first strong observation at that meeting was that what was to be said would not really be important, because evidenced by the jaded behavior of many faculty members, I knew they had all been through this before and knew its lack of value. My second consideration was a reminder that as a teacher, I would be challenged on a daily basis to prevent any of this blase and rude behavior in my classes by making the material and delivery fresh and important in order to stave off boredom, the curse of any teacher's lesson plan.

That first semester I was assigned three classes of English I (called Neanderthal English by one of the wearier members of the department), one class of Basic English III (Sophomore Speech), cafeteria supervision for Lunch hour A from eleven o'clock until eleven-thirty, and helping the debate coach Miss Pratt, by practicing with students to improve their skills for meets. I was also expected to attend the meets on Saturdays and occasionally after school as a judge. At the time, it was overwhelming, but I thought it fair to expect anything from me if they were paying. Now I see that I should have been paid at least three times the salary I was being given.

The night before classes began, I didn't sleep much, even though I tried hard to trust in the education I had been given and in whatever ability I had, which would be tested, not just the next day, but for many years to come. It occurred to me that I had been going to school since I was five years old, and that I would be getting up to "go to school" until my hair was either gray or gone altogether. In any case, the stage was set, and some kind of drama was ready to unfold in my classroom the next day.

Chapter 3 Onward and Upward

It was Wednesday morning at seven when Bob Birchard picked me up in his red MG convertible. As it was early September, the weather was still fairly warm, so we both wore light-weight jackets, and the car's top was down. I carried with me only my notebook of the first week's lesson plans, and a thermos of coffee. Bob had with him the sophomore literature book he would be using for all his classes for the first six weeks, the length of time for each grading period, totaling three for each semester. His classes were all "regular," a term which forever escaped my clear understanding, but which indicated in some way the very standardized materials in use for middle-of-the-road students.

I had already been informed by Miss Mason that my sophomore English class was "basic," which somehow was supposed to describe students of lower language ability from former testing. She added that such classes also often included students with behavior problems. There were no other labels used at that time for the myriad learning disabilities that would trickle through our classes over the coming years, including Attention Deficit Disorder (A.D.D.). Despite a fleet of counselors downstairs, there were really no standard ways to address cases of severe emotional stress for students until someone threw a chair through a window or punched a teacher. Counselors were there mainly to schedule students for classes, not to provide professional advice for the emotionally troubled, except to talk with them and to listen to their problems before sending them back to class.

We arrived at the school's front parking lot just before 7:30, where the doors would open to allow students to go to designated (in letters already sent to parents) areas to pick up their schedules. The first day would be only a half-day, just to meet teachers and to pick up text books. Thursday would be the first full day of classes.

As Bob parked, a group of eight students walked up to us as we were getting out of the car. They were all nicely dressed, and clean-cut enough to visit David and Ricky at Ozzie and Harriet's house for cookies and milk. Two of the boys in the group said how "cool" they thought the car was, and one of the girls then asked if we were teachers. Considering all that gray, white and tinted-blue hair I had seen at the first faculty meeting, I supposed that these kids might either more easily identify with teachers closer to their own ages, or possibly see us as easy marks, because we were new to the system, and as novices, might be more flexible in the educational scheme of things. As it turned out, they were all upperclassmen of some high repute in the school hierarchy, based upon age, intelligence, and general merit. They were all college-bound, showing that easy confidence of people who know where they've been and where they're going. Suddenly, I felt more confidence and hope in myself and my situation as a newcomer. Maybe teaching was going to work out after all, especially if my students turned out to be anything like these paragons of politeness I had just met in the school parking lot.

Entering the building, I saw many other students, mostly in little groups, winding their ways through the crowd to the gym, library, and auditorium, where their counselors were waiting to distribute schedules. The enrollment that semester was over 2300, and it seemed that every one of the students was in the hallway that morning, including obviously new students, who needed direction to their areas. My heart went out to them first. I congratulated myself on identifying the ones I was pretty sure were freshmen, because they looked as bewildered as I felt. The point for me at that moment was that I did know how they felt, and I knew that such a bond would help me for however many years I taught in order to guide those who felt somehow lost.

It felt good to open with my own key room 248, which was filled with sunlight from the south windows overlooking the football field. Then I stood in the hallway just outside my door to greet my sophomore homeroom students as they entered the room. This had been recommended in one of my methods classes as a way to make students feel welcome. As they all streamed into the room reluctantly, I had time to note the variety of haircuts and clothing for all thirty kids. A few of the boys wore flared slacks, that would eventually become full-fledged bell bottoms by the end of the school year. At least half of the girls wore their hair in the style currently sported by singers, Petula Clark and Barbra Streisand, short in back but longer on one side, swept over one ear. One boy with hair over his eyes was wearing a bright plaid shirt that was in serious collision with slacks of a different color and different plaid.

A couple of the boys looked as though they'd been around the block a few times. They had five o'clock shadows that made them look like Long Shoremen or old enough to be on the faculty and ready for tenure. I had the group fill out the white school enrollment cards and then passed out the book rental forms. I told them that for the first day they could sit wherever they liked but that a seating chart would be made to help me keep better track of the 150 students who would be in that room daily. There were a few announcements over the pubic address system, read by the assistant principal, Paul Poteja, who looked like Spiro Agnew but whom students referred to as Mr. Potato Head. He always ended the daily announcements with a "thought for today," which was actually a series of epigrams from boxes of Salada Tea Bags. I remember for some reason the one for that day. "You can always see through people, who make spectacles of themselves." There was no talking by students. Every eye was on me, waiting to see what I would do next. It made me wonder if my face might be smeared with ditto ink, or my nose was running. It didn't matter. The bell rang, and they were all gone as if by magic.

My first period English I class arrived quietly as I stood again outside the classroom door. When I entered the room, they were all seated, only a few whispering, all eyes on me as I went to my desk and stood there for a moment to look back at them. I'll never forget seeing those faces, knowing that however many classes I would teach over however many years, this was my first class, not as a student teacher, but as the real thing. I can still name some of the students from that class and recall how they looked that first day.

There was a partly suppressed group-groan (something we teachers have heard a zillion times) when I said there would be regular and fair homework assignments, but a couple students smiled when they saw my smiling reaction to that groan. I then read the class list aloud, stumbling over some of the long ethnic ones, like Sally Wojtankowski. When you're standing in front of a classroom, it seems that there are many names like Macghilleseatheanaich, which I believe may be Welsh. One boy corrected me when I called out his name, "Raffle," which was the spelling on the class list. "No, Mr. Bolinger. My name is 'Raphael.'" I looked again at the name on my list, thinking there could have been an error in spelling typed by a secretary. I spelled what was there to him, and he admitted the spelling was correct. "Well," I said. There seems to be a pronunciation problem. 'Raffle' is a kind of lottery with prizes being won by some of the people buying chances. Raphael is the male name you pronounced but spelled the lottery word." The look on his face made me realize that he was not understanding a word I was saying, so I just let it go and continued to pronounce his name "Raphael" the rest of the term. Other goofs in pronunciation were undoubtedly my fault, at times triggering slight tittering from the back of the room.

Then I had them fill out class enrollment cards and before collecting them, went around the room to pass out the grammar and literature books, marking serial numbers on their cards and initialing the books and finally having students sign them. I told the class to read for the next day the short story called "The Piece of String" by Guy de Maupassant, the French equivalent of our own O'Henry. The next moan was not as suppressed as the first had been, but the bell rang, and they all left the room quietly as I went back to my desk to take a deep breath and to realize that I had just met the first class of whatever career I would have in teaching. Images from the movie BLACKBOARD JUNGLE began to fade away, but though I felt grateful and more hopeful, I told myself that I shouldn't be too hasty in supposing that every hour of every future day would be as gratifying as homeroom and first period had been.

Second period was Basic English III, the sophomore speech class. I could tell as I stood in the hall greeting these students that they were a much tougher crowd than the freshmen, contrary to what I had been taught, that the behavior of freshmen was only one step above that of chimpanzees, and that because sophomores were above freshmen in the hierarchy, they were able to look down upon freshmen, having achieved a more advanced sense of decorum. Their faces, as I stood before them, told me the story of school having dulled their enthusiasm to the point of their becoming jaded and simply tired of it all. Some had their heads down on desk tops before I even spoke so that I told them all to sit up for the half hour they would be with me that day and that if they could survive that time, they might just make it through the semester.

My mispronouncing of a couple of surnames from the class list, instead of bringing quiet titters from the back row, brought mean and disgusted-looking smirks and unabashed grunts of disapproval from at least half the group. My heart sank for a moment, but I continued by handing out the speech books and having students fill out the enrollment cards with the books' serial numbers. When I said there would be no homework the first night, there was an enthusiastic cheer from most of the class.

I observed as they were leaving, that the haircuts for several of the boys, and nearly all the girls were long enough in front to cover their eyes, at least partially, as if they wanted or needed little curtains behind which to hide. It told me something about how they viewed themselves and how they thought the world saw them. Unlike the freshman girls, these sophomore females wore heavy eye make-up, which didn't really bother me, and there was nothing in the school dress code that banned make-up, as long as it didn't interfere with school work.

My lunchtime duty in the cafeteria came before my own half-hour lunch, and it was what I feared most during the school day. I had never witnessed a food fight, but legends about them having occurred in other cafeterias persisted in my memory, and though I shared lunchtime supervision with Miss Pratt, a three-year veteran speech teacher and debate coach, I cringed at the thought of such a piece of anarchy ever happening during my watch. As it turned out, there were four or five trays left on tables after lunch instead of their being taken to the tray-return window, and I caught one boy throwing a dill pickle at another table, where it hit a young lady on her head before falling to the floor. I wrote him up and sent him to the office of the dean of discipline, Mr. Powers, an ex-Marine sergeant, whose office smelled like a smokehouse from his cigars and whose loud, gruff voice struck fear into even the most recalcitrant students. Detention slips from Mr. Powers fell like autumn leaves upon those who failed to follow the rules, and each morning before school and every afternoon after school the detention room was filled with convicts who had tested the system and come up short by tangling with this terrifying man.

That first day there were only two other incidents of note, one an encounter with a freshman named Johnny in my sixth period English I class. His unruly dark hair covered his eyes, which made him seem to be only half there, as I always considered eye-contact of great importance in any communication. His only response to my simple questions, even about his enrollment card, was "I dunno" in a very muffled voice that sounded as though his mouth were filled with part of a down comforter. I didn't press him for better enunciation, as there was really only enough time left to give the reading assignment I had given the other freshman classes, but I had a feeling that Johnny and I might be locking horns later in the year. My only immediate hope was that he could brush back his hair long enough to read the homework assignment.

After most of the students of sixth period had filed out of the room, one girl with long dark, wavy hair tied into two ponytails approached me. Her large brown eyes spoke of sensitivity, as she smiled to reveal an overbite that made her lower lip almost disappear. She handed me a folded sheet of paper and said, "I'm Debbie Brown, Mr. Bolinger. I write lots of poetry and was wondering if you'd read a sample and let me know tomorrow what you think." I thanked her for her willingness to share her work with me and told her that I would be happy to write a comment.

Seventh period was called "conference hour," which meant preparation for grading papers, planning lessons, and phoning parents when necessary. Though I had done very little that day, I felt exhausted, due partly to emotional anxiety from negative anticipation, and from not having slept much the night before. The next day, Thursday, would be much better, because I had already met my students, and none of them that first day had appeared to be psychotic. That thought, though based upon very flimsy information, was a great comfort to me.

I decided during that final hour of the school day to go down to the office of Mr. Powers to make sure the kid I had nabbed throwing a pickle during lunch hour had actually seen Mr. P. Approaching his office, I heard the most cacophonous yelling. I was told by the secretary to go right in anyway, where I sat down to observe Mr. Powers lambasting the boy I had sent to him earlier. The most horrible insults and threats were being spewed forth by Mr. Powers, and the boy cowered in utter shame. Meanwhile, I observed on Mr. P's desk a box of Heather Breeze facial tissues with a tutu-wearing ballerina on the side. Suddenly Mr. Powers took one out of the box and handed it to the blubbering boy before his desk, a pickle-throwing boy who was now in tears. He was made by Mr. P to apologize to me and to say that he would never again misbehave in the lunchroom or anywhere else in the school. The poor boy did this through heavy sobs that made me know I would never have any trouble from him again.

The trip home after school was a breezy one, but the weather was still warm and sunny, so Bob left the top down. The radio was playing Joni Mitchell singing "Chelsea Morning," and my spirit was soaring. I told Bob about Johnny from my sixth period class, but Bob had nothing good or bad to relate about his first day. He seemed perfectly content to let the wind blow through his hair and to hear the radio.

We drove through the neighborhood surrounding the school. It was a typical blue collar part of Northwest Indiana, with mostly well-kept lawns and a few pink plastic flamingos, and only a couple of houses with rusty cars in driveways, or broken old washing machines on sagging wooden porches.

My college senior-year idealism was still in tact, and I told myself that students needed to understand that education was a way to escape places where they didn't feel happy. It was a way to go where they could be fulfilled, useful, and happy. This reasoning ignored, of course, the fact that in the 1960's the steel mills were still in full vigor, and that many boys would land steady, well-paying jobs, even before graduating from high school, so that reading things like LASSIE, COME HOME, or diagramming sentences for English grammar provided no apparent connection to "making a living," which was the most important and most practical goal in a steel mill town, where pragmatic choices usually trumped idealistic ones, mainly because of dollar signs, at least when it came to education. Most boys looked at their fathers, uncles, and grandfathers, working on the cold strips and in open hearths of the mills and thought that following in those footsteps was their only choice.

Girls were still on shaky ground before the Equal Rights Amendment was passed. Betty Friedan had made an important stride for women in her book THE FEMININE MYSTIQUE, but teenage girls in Northwest Indiana (and elsewhere) still believed that wearing the right hairstyle, eye make-up, and clothing would validate their lives for the only purpose society still offered through marriage and having children, just as most of their mothers had done. America was on the brink of a powerful feminist movement, but most of my female students in 1969-1970 were as yet unaware of the options that were coming to them.

At dinner that evening my parents wanted to know everything about my first day of school. It was like being in kindergarten all over again, though I know they meant well. Their interest was gratifying, but I couldn't help thinking that as an employed young man, I needed an apartment and car of my own. That thought began to intensify in the form of a growing desire for independence.

When I went upstairs, I sat on my bed with the folder I had brought home from school in order to look again at the plans I had for Thursday's classes. A folded piece of notebook paper fell out and onto the floor. It was Debbie's poem, the one for which she had asked for my opinion. I opened it to read only the first four lines, which were written in typical female freshman style, huge looped letters, and each "i" dotted with a little heart.

"How do I love thee? Let me count the ways.
I love thee to the depth and breadth and height
my soul can reach, when feeling out of sight
for the ends of being and ideal grace."

As I read the lines, I remembered Debbie's big, brown eyes, her smile with the overbite, and her timid sincerity. I simply put my head in my hands, laughing and weeping at the same time.

Chapter 4 "I Dunno"

The next day during homeroom I began collecting book rental and was surprised at how many students brought cash instead of checks. My brain became a festival of arithmetic through adding and subtracting for that big, brown envelope. That was a time before pocket calculators were less than $189, and book rental collection with its record keeping responsibility was just one more job placed upon the already tired shoulders of teaching staff. It was recommended that we turn in to the main office each afternoon any book money turned in that day. We as teachers were responsible for the money. Like the other new teachers, fresh out of college and flat broke, I didn't always turn in the cash after school, just the checks, keeping a personal record of what I had borrowed and would be putting back into the envelope before the deadline, which would come after our first payday in two weeks. I used the money, not for any frivolous purpose, but for things like lunch, gas for my ride to and from work, toothpaste, shaving cream, and a haircut. None of this did much for my ego, but I blamed necessity (which would never hold up in a courtroom) on my stealthy behavior.

It seemed that most of my freshmen had read the short story, "The Piece of String" I had given as homework the day before. After a brief written quiz over the story, I posed questions to engage the class in a discussion on the story's purpose and meaning. The theme is the damage an ugly rumor can cause, even over a period of many years. Though the setting of the story is a rural, 19th Century French village, the circumstances carried over to school life, which is a kind of community too. The conflict in which the main character finds himself registered with students already familiar with the cruel and lasting dangers of even petty rumors (something many teens live for). In the story a man's life is destroyed by such a rumor that grows over time. The reader's sympathy is with the main character, Maitre Hauchecome, who rightfully defends his innocence to no avail for years over false accusations based upon faulty interpretation instead of hard evidence. The lack of trust among townspeople, who are willing, even anxious to believe the worst, creates an atmosphere of suspicion that makes the village an awful place for everyone to live.

The class identified parallels between life in that little village and life as a student in a school setting. In their comments, students used words like, fairness, justice, lies, judging, proof, and meanness. I was so proud of the way they approached the theme, identified it, and then related the conflicts to their own experiences. All three classes did this, making me feel like doing cartwheels in the hallway after each session.

A minor issue occurred in third period, when one boy, Sam, raised his hand to say that in his book there was a different author listed for that story. When I asked who was in his book (thinking there might actually have been some sort of misprint), he answered, "Guy something or other," his pronunciation of the first name being with a hard "g" followed by a long "i" as in "guy and gal." When I pronounced it the French way (hard "g" followed by a long "e"), he looked more confused. When I continued, he raised his hand again to say, "It says Guy in my book." his pronunciation hadn't changed at all. When I explained again the French pronunciation, he raised his hand yet again with the most puzzled facial expression and asked, "Are you SURE?" That was when something in my brain snapped, and I indulged in some perfectly shameless sarcasm by saying, "OK, Sammy. You got me. I made the whole thing up just to put one over on you. You may pronounce Monsieur de Maupassant's first name in whatever way makes you happy. My only request is that you spell it correctly." It appeared by the look on his face that even my sarcasm had just flown right over his head, but it didn't matter. I felt better.

The only real downer in all three freshman classes was once again with Johnny in sixth period, who continued to depend upon his response of "I dunno" to any and every question, his dark and full head of hair covering his eyes, as though he didn't want to see or be seen. As he shuffled out of the room at the end of class that day, I realized it might be time for me to contact his parents, but I decided to wait a few more days before making the phone call, so that he wouldn't see me as a narc. It was Debbie standing before my desk after class, who was my next challenge.

We had only five minutes before Debbie would have to be in her seventh period biology class, so I tried to distill my comments on plagiarism into the gentlest but clearest message. I told Debbie that the poem was superb, and I congratulated her on her excellent taste. Then I added that Elizabeth Barrett Browning would not appreciate the unauthorized claim of its creation by a freshman girl over a century later. Debbie seemed surprised that "Sonnets from the Portuguese" had been written to Robert Browning and was one of the most famous collections of poems in the English language.

Debbie's defense was that she had been inspired by the sonnet but that what she had given me was not really Mrs. Browning's. When I asked for some clarification, Debbie replied that in the fourth line of the Browning poem, the words, "being" and "grace" were capitalized, but that in Debbie's "own poem," they were not. Though shocked by her feeble attempt at being acquitted of blatant theft, I was not exactly speechless. I explained it in terms of stealing, which in many cases would have legal consequences. I paused for just a moment as I looked over at the big brown envelope for book rental still on my desk and then continued.

As I had already gone overtime in my comments, I wrote Debbie a pass to her seventh period while ending my mini-lecture in saying that I was much more interested in reading Debbie's own work, whatever that might be, and that in future I would be very happy to read anything she gave me, as long as she had created it by herself. I told her it was all about creativity and honesty. She then left my classroom, apparently unscathed by anything I had said, and I wondered if the next poem she handed in might be "Shall I compare thee to a summer's day?" At least she stole only from the best.

During conference period that day I graded the quizzes over "The Piece of String" and was generally pleased that most of the students had read the assignment, but when I got to the papers for period six, I was astonished by Johnny's paper, which showed his name, the date, and English I written neatly where they were supposed to be, in the upper right-hand corner. For all ten answers, however, he had written, "I don't know," something I would certainly have deduced, had he not bothered to write it. The real shock, though, came when I turned the paper over to see a drawing of me. Not only was it labeled, "Mr. Bolinger," but it actually looked like me, I mean REALLY like me, except that in the drawing my right arm was in a sling, there were stitches along my forehead, and I was on crutches. Also there was a cartoon bubble from my mouth that said, "Do your homework!" It was obvious by the skill of the drawing itself that the problem I had seen before involved a much more complex and talented young man than I had imagined. It was time for me to do something before things got worse.

Because it was only 2:40, I decided to phone Johnny's parents to see if they could be my allies in helping Johnny find a different purpose for being in my class. I had as yet never heard him say anything but, "I dunno" in the most muffled voice. I felt terrible that I had somehow got off on the wrong foot with him, or he with me, but I thought things could be set right if his parents could help by encouraging him to do his work and shoot for a diploma instead of a protective order from the police.

From the school enrollment card I got Johnny's phone number and placed the call in the English Department office. I waited for five rings before someone picked up the receiver but saying nothing. I heard breathing, so I spoke first. "Hello. May I please speak to Mrs. Madison?"

"Uh huh," came the response.

"This is Mr. Bolinger at Morton High School, Mrs. Madison, and I'm calling about your son Johnny, who's in my sixth period English I class, where he seems to be having some kind of struggle doing his work. You know him best, so I'm hoping that as a team you and I can talk with him so he can get on the right track to getting a credit for the semester."

There was an uncomfortable silence.

"Hello. Mrs. Madison? Are you still there?"

"Uh huh," she repeated.

"Well, can you help me get Johnny working on getting that credit?"

"I dunno," she said before hanging up.

At that moment I had a vision of the Madisons' family life at home, complete with grunting relatives wearing bear skins and throwing table scraps to a pack of wild dogs roaming through their dining room food pit. I knew in any case that the problem might just be genetic and that I had a battle of epic proportions ahead of me.

Chapter 5 "When I Break Outta Here"

Like most classes of freshmen, the three groups of them I had that semester became much less timid as the weeks passed, feeling more at ease in their surroundings, and becoming bolder in their occasional whispering and passing of notes during class. The shy, frightened, and overwhelmed kids from early September were already beginning to see themselves as veterans in a system from which they knew there was no real escape, but in which they also knew they could survive with just enough deception to get by on homework, school rules they saw as oppressive, and to pacify some parents and teachers in order to receive credits toward eventual graduation, perhaps the ultimate escape. The scary part for me was that I remembered being a high school freshman and being just like most of the students I was teaching.

The basic sophomore speech class, much more hardened by school and by life itself, was a tremendous challenge each day. The wall they had been building up against formal education was now at least six feet thick and twenty feet high, so that my scaling or getting through it would take all the energy, guile, and compassion that I had. It all meant making my class, not only more entertaining, but more significant. A common phrase among them was, "when I break outta here," which meant leaving at age sixteen to work somewhere, or graduating with a diploma. In at least a couple of cases, boys escaped the "prison" of high school only to spend years in actual jails for theft and assault and battery. I suddenly understood how parents must feel in their sometimes heroic attempts to keep their children on productive paths and out of trouble.

As tough as their manners appeared, some of the class were still terrified of getting up in front of their peers, or anyone else, to speak. My goal was to get every student to feel prepared and comfortable in front of a group. Some of the same ones, who had phobias of speaking in front of the class, were among the loudest and most enthusiastic cheerers at football games, so I knew there was an energy and fearlessness inside them that could be tapped for use in the classroom.

I told the class that speaking in front of groups brought fear shared by many others, but that overcoming it could bring great benefits, especially to those among them who might end up being managers or foremen in their places of work. I added that leaving the path open to opportunities and preparing for a wide range of employment choices was a good thing for everybody. I said that I wanted them all to be ready for the best jobs, the ones they would enjoy the most and that would offer the best benefits, which often meant positions of leadership, requiring the ability and courage to speak comfortably before groups. I noticed that the word, "courage" perked up the attention of some of the boys, for whom bravery was probably the most important quality anyone could possess. It was, as usual, difficult to tell if I was making any real headway, but I continued by giving the first speech assignment.

I said that the next day I wanted everyone to stand at the podium in front of the rest of the class just to say his or her name, and to identify a favorite pastime or hobby, even if only a television program, and explain for just a minute or two its personal appeal. There were some tossing heads, and rolling eyes, but the assignment had been given. The deed had been done. Pete and Dierdre, the ones who were usually the most critical of any demands I made of the class, sat in the back of the room, wearing smirks that made them look like the most judgmental man and wife preparing to give a new son-in-law their lowest opinion of him. The bell rang, and everyone left, except Dierdre, who told me that it would be much too difficult for her to speak in front of a group about anything positive, since she hated EVERYTHING. At first, I thought she might be kidding, but the look in her eyes communicated absolute sincerity. My response was that she was welcome to talk about something she disliked, as long as she gave some clear explanation about her aversion. She looked at me for what seemed a long time before smiling, nodding, and leaving the room. Had I given her carte blanche to turn my assignment upside down? I couldn't tell.

The freshmen were reading another story by Guy de Maupassant, "The Necklace," a masterpiece of irony. I also gave an assignment to create five examples of situational irony, that is whatever showed a shocking contradiction between what was true and what only seemed to be true. The students did well, except for two duplicate sets from first period, indicating that one kid had simply copied from the other. Neither received credit for the homework. However, the rest of the students in all three English I classes came up with good examples, like, an award-winning dentist whose daughter has a mouth filled with cavities, a jet pilot with a phobia of heights, a mass murderer, who wins the Nobel Prize for Peace, a concert pianist, who can't play the song, "Happy Birthday," and a summer snow storm in Miami, Florida. There were many more, which I can't remember, but I read them aloud, to the pleasure of each class. I ended my unit on irony by assigning three short stories by America's master of irony, O'Henry, through his, "Cop and the Anthem," The Ransom of Red Chief," and "The Gift of the Magi." The most popular among students was "Ransom." I was hoping students would begin to recognize irony in real life too. Our class discussions on the stories were lively, and showed genuine interest by most. I was feeling especially good about all that until a boy named Dan in first period said loudly enough for all to hear, "This is stupid. Why do we have to read stories about things that aren't even true? That's all fiction is, ain't it?"

I felt my spirit shrink for a moment, but after reminding Dan about trying not to use "ain't," especially in an English class, I explained that life itself, for everybody, felt stupid at times, and that stories of fiction, if they were worth anything, dealt with emotional truths of human behavior in all its splendor and weakness too, and that we could all learn a lot from the triumphs and mistakes of literary characters, who may not be in Dan's phone book reality, but very real in the psychological sense of actual human values and behavior in all its fascinating patterns of good and evil, and everything in between. At times like those, I would often stop for a moment, close my eyes, and wonder if I was teaching or merely pontificating. I wanted so much for all my students to find purpose and meaning in literature, which had been such a wonderful refuge for me since the age of four, but I came only gradually to realize that reaching all thirty students in any classroom at the same time was a rare accomplishment, perhaps even a miracle, and in darker moments, I even allowed myself the idea that we may hope for or suspect many things, but we know almost nothing.

The period ended with three girls, all named Tiffany, raising their hands energetically to say that they loved the stories we were reading and liked our discussions too. One of the girls added that she thought Danny was stupid. I was about to curtail what might have turned into a verbal brawl (by the surprised and then angry look on Dan's face), but the bell saved us all, as it so often did, and I felt some glimmer of hope in what the girls had said about liking the stories.

The first little "speeches" given by my sophomores went well in the sense that everyone present participated, even if the material was duller than a butter knife trying to cut through raw turnips. They all knew at least that they could speak in front of a group without fainting. Deirdre's speech was articulate, even though her subject was based upon her complete hatred of giving speeches (more irony!). She backed up her topic with reasons and examples, and received an "A." The next ones would be demonstration speeches, each one between two and five minutes, explaining how to perform some task, giving clear steps to completing whatever the job was.

The next day there were the usual demo speeches about how to make ice box cookies, a trivet with Pop-Cicle sticks, how to put on eye shadow and eye liner, how to organize a scrap book, how to apply a tourniquet, and how to perform the Heimlich Maneuver, for which I was the make-believe but hapless victim. It was the demo speech on karate given by Jim Davis that I remember most clearly. Jim was already a Black Belt, who actually taught an evening karate class in downtown Hammond two nights a week. Jim was a stout, solid-looking kid of quiet but determined demeanor. He had already brought me a note signed by both his parents giving their permission for Jim to break a pine board with his bare hand for his speech that day. Despite mental images of Jim's broken hand, and having to call the school nurse and possibly an ambulance, followed by a long class interruption that the rest of the students would undoubtedly relish, I consented, even if reluctantly. What can I say? I was a first-year teacher, anxious, even desperate for my classes to be more exciting and interesting. In any case, I had thrown the dice. Now we were all about to see the results.

Jim asked for two assistants to hold the pine plank he intended to break in half by means of one karate chop. Their hands raised high, all the other boys in the class were practically leaping from their seats to volunteer. Even a couple of the girls were anxious to help. Jim prepared us by speaking about how to approach the challenge with deep concentration on at least two levels. He said such things were "mind over matter" and that this endeavor was more mental than physical. As two boys held the board up tightly in the air, Jim closed his eyes in deep concentration, taking a big breath, and moving his hand with lightning speed toward that target, even as my own eyes opened from the prayer I had just whispered. There was a sound of splitting wood, and to my utter and everlasting relief, the two assistants each held half of the original board.

There was no blood or cry of pain, only a look of satisfaction on Jim's face and on the faces of the two amazed boys who had helped him. There was a spontaneous explosion of applause from the rest of the class, including me, and everyone, even Deirdre, stood to acknowledge that we had all witnessed something extraordinary. When things quieted down a bit, I said in a deliberately frightened and hysterical voice, "You get an 'A'!" The class got the joke and burst out laughing. Then the bell rang, and everyone left, except Jim, who thanked me for letting him show his skill. I asked for half of the broken board as a memento, which he even signed for me. That hour I would always remember as a triumph and a joy from my years of teaching.

There was still the problem of Johnny Madison, whose "I dunno" haunted my dreams and continued to make me feel like a failure, at least in sixth period. I hoped that some sign of progress might be on its way, and I was about to find out.

Chapter 6 Free Condiments

Independence was on my mind more and more, especially at breakfast, when Mom would set the bowl of hot oatmeal with banana or strawberries, coffee, and orange juice before me at the dining room table, not my table, but my parents' table. I felt in some ways as though I were still in high school myself, not as a teacher, but as a pupil. The old patterns were still in place, and I was beginning to crave a drastic change in venue. Most of my friends had their own apartments, which made me desirous of sitting in my own living room, listening to music on my own radio, eating in my own kitchen, driving my own car. I loved my parents and was grateful for all the help they had given me, but that sophomore line, "When I break outta here" was becoming more personal for me as autumn came and Indiana trees began to turn gold, scarlet, and amber.

After taxes and my pension deduction, my first pay check was for exactly $226, of which $50 went back into the book rental envelope to replace the money I had borrowed from it. My parents, knowing my wish for a place of my own, refused the $75 that I was scheduled to give them monthly for room and board. That left me with $176 to put aside toward an apartment, but I would need to wait another two weeks for another pay check before putting a deposit on even a studio apartment, but that thought gave me something to look forward to.

Meanwhile, school days moved into the very welcome cooler weather, as the school building was not yet equipped with air conditioning. One afternoon in early September, when temperatures on the second floor had soared into the nineties, school was dismissed for the rest of the day. Part of the problem was that the building had been designed to accommodate air conditioning with sealed windows throughout, windows that could not be opened. When the sun hit the south side of the school, rooms on the second floor often became terrariums of heat and Indiana humidity from Lake Michigan. The job of teaching and that of learning both became quite challenging in a steam bath atmosphere, that by one o'clock sometimes had students draped over their desks, facing instructors, whose neckties were loosened, sleeves rolled up, and who were seated on teacher desk tops, fanning themselves with Manila folders.

The board of education, along with other powers that be, had to decide whether the $150,000 set aside for air conditioning should be used for the installation the year before in 1968. The decision had been made to use the fund instead on lights for the football field. Priorities became perfectly clear. Breathing and remaining conscious in classrooms, it seemed, were not as important as bringing the community together for sports events. Such was the value system when I began teaching, and so it remained for all the years I taught, sports events taking precedence over music, art, or theater events, which existed to a great extent on private contributions and bake sales. Maybe that's because competition with other schools was used in order to flare up "school spirit," that synthetic version of ancient, tribal loyalty that would raise adrenaline for release of excess teenage energy at those thunderous pep sessions in the gym before basketball or football games. It should be remembered that basketball in Indiana is truly a religion, as in practically no other place in the world. In fairness, I should add that even in high school I was a stick in the mud about crowds on bleachers, screaming their lungs out in preparation for a game that mattered to me about as much as the world's record for the biggest ball of string.

Still euphoric from the board-breaking, boredom-smashing sophomore class period from the day before, I was brought back down to earth by an incident in the cafeteria during my lunchtime supervision, when I was making the rounds to make sure all lunch trays were being taken to the return window. Suddenly from the other side of the room, came the sound of dishes hitting the floor, and the deep grumbling of two male voices. Students were already standing on benches and even tables, all their attention directed to the north side of the room, where there was a commons area facing the courtyard garden. At first unable to see anything wrong, I ran toward the commotion, where I found, writhing on the floor, two senior boys, both huge football players, locked together in what appeared to be mortal combat.

As was so often the case, when there were physical battles between students, the noise level was such that a teacher's voice could not be heard, or even if it was, didn't matter one tiny bit. Both boys continued throwing punches and screaming things like, "She's my girl, not yours!" While poor Miss Pratt stood by saying, "Now boys, this won't do at all," I went down on my knees to grab an arm to try pulling one of the boys away from the other. This was, on my part, a useless move, as each boy weighed over two hundred pounds, and the passion of their combined rage blotted out any hope of either boy hearing or caring about anyone's protest to stop the fighting. As is often the case with boys when they fight, saving face meant a lot too. As I was to learn over the years as a teacher, when girls fight, saving face has nothing to do with it. The object is always simply to kill the other girl.

When I saw a spatter of blood on the tile floor, I knew that I had to do something, and fast. While Miss Pratt stood there shivering with fear and continuing to yell, "Enough, boys, enough!" I ran to the condiment table for plastic bottles of ketchup and mustard. Then rushing back to the fray, I tried once more to scream my message that the two separate, "Now!" When there was still no response, and blows continued to be exchanged, I pointed both bottles at the boys and let them have it, squeezing almost all the contents onto their faces and all over their shoulders, right after which one of the boys yelled, "Oh, my God! I'm bleeding!"

"Get up," I said. "It's only ketchup!" Both finally stood, covered by the taxi cab yellow of the hot dog mustard, and the deep red of the ketchup.

There were gales of laughter from crowds of other students as the two seniors headed for the main office, while I pushed the P.A. button on the wall to notify the staff there to nail a couple of big guys covered in condiments. As soon as the bell rang, the crowd from that lunch shift went on to fifth hour, and I headed for the nearest comfortable chair in the teachers' lounge. I skipped lunch, as my appetite had been somewhat compromised by doing battle myself. Both boys received three days of out-of-school suspension. A week or so later, one of them came to thank me for breaking up what he thought might have become a homicide. His mom's only complaint was that the ketchup stains were not coming out of his shirt. Nowadays, I'd probably be thrown in prison. But that was the worst of it, and there seemed to be no hard feelings from either boy afterward toward each other or toward me. For the rest of that school year, I was known as "the mustard and ketchup guy" by students who weren't in my classes.

Another English teacher, Glenn, who over my years at MHS would become a good friend, used to keep a small bucket of fresh water in his classroom, in order to break up fights that couldn't be stopped quickly any other way. He told me never to try breaking up fights between girls. "They're usually in it to the death," he advised me. "And considering those fingernails, and the fact that girls often bite, you could be julienned in seconds." It was advice I never forgot.

The problem of Johnny Madison continued to dominate my thoughts about sixth period. Over the coming years, it was not uncommon for one student in a class to commandeer my concern, often taking my attention away from others in the group. It may have been that my vanity about being able to help turn a kid's attitude around became too much the focus of my efforts. Maybe my almost evangelical zeal came from my sometimes unrealistic view that "I can do this!" Unfortunately, I was not always a success in my attempts to be an Albert Schweitzer or Mother Teresa to students who simply did not want to be helped.

One thing I learned with great difficulty about teaching was that though perseverance was a noble thing, there every once in a while came a case for which even all my efforts were just not enough. Even now, I think that "No Child Left Behind" fails occasionally to take into account those rare but real examples of students, who were not left behind, but rather leaped from the train or never boarded in the first place. The pretense, hypocrisy, and even idealism of public expectation about learning are occasionally blurred in their serious collision with reality.

When I assigned a one-page essay to my freshmen, it was to convey their views on school and being a freshman thus far, expressing too what they wanted to see changed about the current system. This is typical of first-year teachers, and I was no exception. I'm fairly certain that my opening that door of freedom was very common among new teachers, who want their students to feel they have voices that matter. The result of that assignment, besides my learning that freshmen were deficient in their knowledge of paragraphing, grammar, spelling, and punctuation, was that their collective plea was for less homework. I still don't know why I was surprised, but it didn't change my belief that the responsibility of regular homework was important. The first sample of their writing showed me just how much work we all had ahead of us.

It was Johnny's paper which, yet again, managed to stun me. It was two pages long with the title "School." The shock came in seeing the content itself of, "School is stupid, stupid, stupid..." the word, "stupid" repeated enough times to fill the rest of the first page, and all of the second. Johnny had actually spent a lot of time and effort making his point, one that showed a huge amount of angst. All I could come up with for a reason was that his mother had told him I called. My feeling at that stage was also that the Madisons had probably received many phone calls from other teachers over time, whose comments had perhaps not been as relatively gracious as mine had been but that Johnny had lumped them all together so that any call from school must automatically be a threat of punishment.

During my conference hour seventh period that day I phoned Mrs. Madison again, hoping that this time there might be an actual conversation that could point toward mutual cooperation for Johnny's sake. I let the phone ring ten times before giving up. Those were the days before answering machines and voice mail. I even considered paying a visit to Johnny's home, but my vision of walls filled by gun racks gave me pause, so that I decided to wait. Instead, after school I decided to talk with Johnny's other teachers at a scheduled faculty meeting at which the topic for the first twenty minutes was whether cartons of milk in the cafeteria should cost ten or twelve cents. I began to chew the eraser off my pencil in frustration at this apparent waste of valuable time. Despite the seemingly endless forty minutes that had nothing remotely to do with teaching or my problems with Johnny, I managed afterward to catch two of his other teachers, one for biology, and one for algebra. They both told me that he had done nothing in their classes either and that he would probably fail. Like me, they had both mailed deficiency notices to his parents but had heard nothing in response.

Johnny's biology teacher added that she thought Johnny might be very slow, but I told her that I suspected he was quite intelligent, showing her then the drawing of me I had saved. At first looking at me as if I were speaking Swahili, she then stifled what could have been a hearty laugh and asked me to contact her if I heard from Johnny's parents and told me she would let me know too if she heard from them. I thanked both teachers and walked over to Bob, who was waiting near the door, obviously more than ready to leave.

That evening at dinner, Dad told me about an apartment he had heard about that was walking distance from the school and was going for $150 per month.

Chapter 7 The Sound of Bells

It occurred to me one morning as my alarm clock began ringing, that my life was to a great extent, and always had been, controlled by bells. Those were the days before varied and creative ring tones and cell phones. Every hour at school a bell would announce the end of one class and then ring again five minutes later to signal the beginning of the next. There were church bells to proclaim each service, a tolling bell to honor each funeral, pealing clusters of bells for weddings, doorbells signaling that guests had arrived, and bells on fire trucks all over town. The worst was, of course, my alarm clock with its daily and aggravating reminder that choices regarding sleep were limited. Poe's poem, "The Bells" cemented a bond between me and the deceased poet. How well he understood the variety of bells! The other bell that was only in my mind but just as real as the others, was the one used in a boxing match. I sometimes heard it mentally on days when my classroom felt a bit like a boxing ring with rounds of combat over lessons in grammar or spelling.

Catherine Kavin taught Basic English classes all day long in her classroom next to mine. In her late fifties when I began teaching, she had short, silver hair, and a brusque, no-nonsense disposition, which had earned her the nickname of "Sergeant Kavin" from her students. Very strict, and with an almost pathological sense of order, Mrs. Kavin talked out of the right side of her mouth, almost as though she were aiming her words more sharply at some target. Though she was proud of her work "civilizing" her basic freshmen and sophomores, her pride was based mostly upon her military control of her classes. At the same time, she seemed to think that being "basic" was some terrible affliction, and that being "basic" indicated one of the lowest forms of life, somewhere between mollusks and amphibians. Her homeroom was a mixed group of juniors, that included several honors students. When she wanted to reprimand that assemblage, the worst possible put-down in her verbal arsenal was the question, "What are you kids, BASICS?"

The "Sergeant" at that time was, in order to soften her image slightly, experimenting with various wigs she would wear to school. It was obvious she was aware that people would know she was wearing wigs, because the lengths varied too much for anyone to believe that someone's hair could change so drastically from one day to the next. The wigs, though they did soften her appearance, also altered her level of fear factor, rendering her a more comic figure than she had been before.

One of the things Mrs. Kavin did in her classes at least twice a week was to read to her students while sitting, cross-legged, on a conference table. The table had telescope legs that adjusted the height of the table or collapsed completely for storage. The kids reputedly enjoyed the sergeant's oral readings, as she would become the characters in any selections she was using.

One day during third period, my English I class was interrupted by a loud crash from Mrs. Kavin's room. Telling my students to remain in their seats, I rushed next door, to find Mrs. Kavin sitting on the floor, evidently having slid off the table, a leg from which had collapsed, leaving the sergeant with her wig half off, eyeglasses on the floor, her dress up over her left shoulder, slip showing, and a copy of DAVID COPPERFIELD still in her hands.

I helped her up, after which she straightened her wig, putting on her glasses, and continued the oral reading with resumed dignity, where she had stopped before the avalanche. I've never seen a group stifle laughter as successfully as that class did. They had apparently, according to other stories I had heard about Mrs. K, had a lot of practice confining hearty guffaws to inaudible snickers on almost a daily basis. I needed some of that practice myself in order to face Mrs. Kavin forever after, doing my best to avoid her unless I had time to prepare myself.

I passed back the graded essays to my freshmen, with two sets of points on each, half for mechanics and grammar, and the other half for content. I had to fight off a very strong inclination to write, "This is stupid" on Johnny Madison's paper, deciding finally that even if fighting fire with fire might have a powerful effect, it was rather unprofessional. I wrote instead, "Johnny, you are capable of so much more than this." It was, I suppose, a coward's comment, based upon my fear that antagonizing Johnny could completely destroy any possible trust and respect between us, trust and respect being essentials in the teaching game, perhaps more important than text books, pencils, chalk boards, or air conditioning. In that respect, I felt that my honor was at stake. It seemed as though my worth as a teacher was on the line, and that if I could reach Johnny, I could reach anybody.

Deirdre, in my second hour Basic English III class, was another challenge, but at least she communicated what she thought and made it clear why she felt as she did. Johnny remained apparently unwilling to share any reasons for his evident hatred of school. Having talked with his other teachers, I felt certain that his intense dislike of school was not directed at me personally. Maybe he hated the whole world, and my English class was just a tiny fragment of that grand animosity. At any rate, I wasn't going to give up without a fight.

Mid-October became quite chilly, but the southern exposure of my sunny classroom assured that in cold weather we would have a better chance of staying comfortable than rooms on the north side of the building. Homeroom was the only part of the day that was sometimes cold, because the room needed more time to warm up. That mild and brief discomfort was compounded slightly by Mr. Poteja's regular "thought for today" messages, which sometimes left us all wearing puzzled looks from the mystery of the epigram's significance. A case in point was, "Thought for today: Throw down your hammers, and pick up your shovels." From the back of my classroom came a whisper of, "What the hell does THAT mean?" I didn't feel that I knew any more how to answer that question than anyone else on the planet, and besides, I was biting my tongue to keep from laughing aloud.

The school was preparing for an open house to welcome parents after the first six weeks of classes. We on the faculty were encouraged to spruce up our classroom bulletin boards, and to have our grade books ready to back up any comments we might have about a student's progress. The PTA prepared a generous pot luck supper for faculty and staff. This included a wonderful dessert table with a scrumptious lemon meringue pie.

Over thirty people, mostly couples, but a few single mothers, one father, and even a grandmother, came to talk with me about their kids. These were the people, who really wanted to know about the progress of their children and how they, as guardians, could help to motivate at home to help kids do their best. In this beginning of a pattern that would persist all the years I taught, the parents whom I wanted and needed most to see were not there, even though I kept watching for the parents of students like, Pete, Deirdre, and especially Johnny. I was learning what an essential role family played in the education of kids. The anchors of concern, discipline, and, most importantly, encouragement, were needed but absent in so many homes, as the burden shifted more and more toward the school to be surrogate motivators.

Armed with a big slice of lemon meringue pie, wrapped in aluminum foil by Mrs. Rafferty, president of the PTA, I turned out the light in my classroom, looking once more at the bulletin board on "Irony" prepared by my freshmen. Almost everyone else was gone by nine o'clock, but I had stayed, harboring the hope of meeting the Madisons.

If I were asked today by a beginning teacher how to motivate students, I would feel more qualified to answer than I would have felt during that autumn of 1969, when in my mind was the clash between all those college classes on theory of method and management versus the reality of my being in the trenches. Now I would say that individualization is, of course, important, but that the most prominent need is to arouse and keep one's own passion for learning. The excitement a teacher generates comes from deep within himself first, not from some textbook. His love of a story, or even a lesson on punctuation will be infectious. If he hates THE SCARLET LETTER, his students will pick up on this, and he will not inspire them to love it either.

Humor used in small doses can break the ice during many conflicts. Though a teacher is not a stand-up comic, or a substitute for MTV, he will succeed more often if there is a sense that he doesn't take himself too seriously all the time. Sometimes kids can learn more from Bart Simpson than from Ernest Hemingway. Cajoling has its place too (i.e. "Do your homework. I know where you live.")

The morning after open house, when my alarm rang its hateful little bell, instead of feeling resentful of its harsh sound, I bolted up in bed, my first thought being, "Today is pay day." There was suddenly the sweet smell of freedom in the air.

Chapter 8 Faculty Feuds, and Freedom

A school faculty is its own little community of factions as varied as religious denominations. As a new teacher, I had the chance to observe from a safe distance the miniature solar system that existed in that universe, called a public high school.

I was amazed at how seemingly departmental the faculty friendships were. Of course, it's probably reasonable to assume that friends share interests, but it struck me as odd that such relationships on our faculty appeared often to be limited to areas of study, which were further segregated by being clustered together in parts of the building devoted to social studies, English, foreign language, (which I was unhappy to discover included English), math, science, physical education, music, and art. Some of the divisions made perfect sense, like those last three I mentioned. Such grouping for other departments escaped me though, except in terms of keeping materials for each in a separate area.

In the teachers' cafeteria/lounge, there were areas of unspoken but definite designation for certain departments. For example, as there were no women in the social studies department, a large conference table was protected territorially by a group of men, who taught world geography, economics, government, world history, and American history. That table remained a separate area, in which I was sometimes surprised that the men didn't just pee on their chairs to mark their territory. Women hung purses and other bags over chairs to mark their own territories. The social studies table was further protected by an orb of cigarette and cigar smoke, penetrated by only one female outsider, Mrs. Graham, the flirtatious teacher of French. Her flattery and cajoling gave her access to that little kingdom ruled by Mr. Clifford Potts, a white-haired and overweight relic from the 1920's, whose reactionary views would have shocked even Barry Goldwater. Mr. Potts always sat at the head of that table, like the patriarch at a Thanksgiving dinner, or a monarch for whom others were expected to pay court.

The World Geography teacher, Mr. Jack Farrel, was known, and in some quarters feared, for his caustic and often stinging wit, directed at any passers-by, at students, and especially at anyone, who dared to disagree with his ego-maniacal view that the world was being destroyed by new and subversive notions of the young. In my listening encounters (eavesdropping), I knew him only once to be stumped in delivering the proper insult or other put-down. This particular barb was intended for Mrs. Helen Warren, a charming, intelligent, and kind woman from the business department, though she was not present for this verbal exchange. At the social studies table one afternoon someone commented that no one really liked the new choir director. Someone else said, "Helen likes him and thinks he'll do a lot for the music department." Jack's usual attempt to provide an acidic comment to end the conversation failed this time in his saying, "Yes, but Helen likes EVERYONE." From the lunch tray window, having heard and seen the whole thing, I could observe in his face the terrible realization that, for once, he had inadvertently given a kind of compliment, instead of his usual verbal harpoon. It was one of those classic moments of virtue's triumph over vice. In later years, Jack would become known as the Darth Vader of the faculty, and at Christmas time, he was always referred to, at least behind his back, as the embodiment of The Grinch. Talk about type-casting!

There was also a government teacher, Mr. Rutland who always came to school early enough each morning to cover all his chalk boards with his notes for the day, which all his classes copied dutifully into their notebooks for future quizzes and exams. This was how they spent their time in his class, never hearing a lecture or engaging in a discussion or debate. One year at a faculty Christmas party, Mr. Rutland received a "Dead Sea Scrolls" trophy for having and using the oldest ditto masters, some of which one wag claimed went back to the time of President Taft. It was only a gag gift, but Mr. Rutland was livid and stomped out of the party, red-faced and unable to return to the festivities.

Then there was another government teacher, Mr. Clinton, who walked around his classroom, lecturing passionately and interestingly, challenging students in surprise ways, with stimulating questions, encouraging debate, and lots of discussion. Now in his seventies, he's still there, someone I was always proud to call my colleague. Teaching is in his blood.

The math department opted for a large round table, most appropriate, because there were two women in the group, creating some sense of balance in talk that was always more varied and liberal than that from the social studies guys. The math people were always welcoming of those from other departments, who might join them for lunch. Those math teachers were also always happy to hear of anything going on in the outside world, which meant anything happening in some other academic department.

Members of the music, P.E., and science departments rarely made appearances in the faculty lunch room, as there was always extra time needed for rehearsing for concerts, monitoring free throws in the gym, or backstrokes in the pool, or preparing for science fairs. The dedication of those teachers included bringing sack lunches and thermoses of coffee or tea to get through a day that, for them, was usually longer than that for the rest of the staff.

The most hospitable and liberal faculty table at lunch was that of the English and foreign language departments, whose tables were always put beside each other to accommodate at least ten people at once. I suppose I like the adjectives, "hospitable" and "liberal," because I was a member of bother groups and enjoyed the exhilaration of talking about the latest books, films, restaurants, and gossip, instead of just football, even though I also enjoyed eavesdropping on the other planets of our little solar system.

At that time I was teaching my freshmen how to diagram sentences. Many still think that this technique is old-fashioned, but it does provide an effective, visual way to understand how a sentence is built from the ground up. For the boys it was like reducing the words to pieces in an Erector Set. The relationships between words became more dependable. I believe my students understood grammar better after being able to identify every part of a sentence and its connection to every other part. We had contests at the chalk board between teams, drawing sentences written on little folded pieces of paper from a big wooden salad bowl, and the puzzle nature of grammar in this way became more entertaining. Miss Mason, our department chair, encouraged me to remain devoted to teaching the mechanics and structure of language.

A problem arose one day, when one of my freshmen raised her hand to say that her biology teacher, Mr. Matthews, had said that diagramming sentences was a "ridiculous waste of time." Ellen seemed quite shaken that my zeal in teaching this skill had been openly criticized by another teacher, whom she also respected, a teacher, however, who didn't know me but who had seen Ellen diagramming sentences in his biology class and had become unhinged, making an unnecessarily ugly issue of the whole thing through his thoughtless statement.

I thanked Ellen for the information but said nothing in class about my feelings, one way or another. After school, however, I went straight to Mr. Matthews' room to confront him and find out if he had actually said what had been relayed to me. When he admitted saying exactly what I had been told he said, I told him that though he had a perfect right to dispute the value of sentence diagramming, he had shown poor taste and judgment by undermining my efforts to teach grammar. I added that I would in future appreciate his coming directly to me in order to ask why I was doing certain things in my lessons, so that I could ease his mind by giving him sound reasons for my actions. When he tried to brush aside what he had said as totally unimportant, I put to him a hypothetical case of my saying to his students in my class that studying chromosomes or blood circulation was an utter waste of time, and ridiculous into the bargain. I asked if he wouldn't feel that his efforts were being subverted. His bold and apparently insincere response was that he didn't know. Before leaving, I told him that what he had said was unethical and unprofessional, and that mutual support among faculty was extremely important to us all. Finally, he smiled and apologized, adding that it would never happen again. We even shook hands as I thanked him, but I don't think our paths ever crossed again.

During conference period one afternoon, I finally made a telephone connection with the Madison house. It was Johnny's father, who answered, surprising me, like an unexpected but pleasantly cold gust of wind on a hot day. His voice, unlike his wife's, was articulate and reassuring. I told him that if his coming to the school was a problem, that I could visit his home instead, in order to talk about Johnny. After four o'clock on the following Monday was the time we set for my visit to the Madison home. Johnny would be at swimming practice that day until five. I didn't want to practice any subterfuge, but Johnny was in real danger of failing the semester, so I felt no guilt in setting up a meeting behind his back. Having heard Mr. Madison's rational voice, I breathed a sigh of relief that some sort of progress for his son might be just around the corner.

By mid-November I had my fifth pay check, and Bob drove me after school to an apartment rental office, where I inquired about the one-bedroom second-floor place at the Williamsburg Square complex just a block from school. The agent said she would take me there and then drive me home, so I thanked Bob and sent him on his way.

The agent and I walked up a flight of stairs to apartment 2C at 3618 Vine Street, among of a set of blond brick buildings surrounding a large parking lot with clean landscaping of flowers and manicured lawns. She pointed out the generous picture window of my apartment facing south, as well as the little balcony over the downstairs entrance. She opened the door to reveal a twelve by sixteen living room of warm, gold, sculptured carpeting, and cream-colored walls. There was a wall-unit air conditioner in that room. The kitchen was separated only by a four-foot-high wood bookcase. In the kitchen there was room for a table and probably four chairs. An electric range, a fridge, a small pantry,and a wall of oak cabinets completed that room. The tiny bathroom had a little closet for linens and a large tub with shower. There were no windows on the north side of the place. The same white vinyl tile floor was in both the kitchen and bath areas. The bedroom was the size of the living room and had a set of eye-level windows on the south side, and a large closet with folding doors.

The agent was patient and understood, I think, that this was my first apartment and how much it meant to me. By the time we left, the sun was pouring in through the bedroom and living room windows onto that gold carpeting. It was easy for me to see myself living there, on my own, independent at last. I think the agent saw all this in my face and could sense my mental planning already of having dinner guests and loving the space as my own home. Before she took me home, we stopped by her office for me to sign the contract, pay the deposit and first month's rent, the total for both being $300, which at the time was a small fortune to me, but well worth what I was getting in return. I will never forget her handing me the three keys, one for the apartment, one for the laundry room, and one for the shed, where I would be keeping my bicycle. For the first time (age twenty-three) I felt that I was an adult, even if I didn't yet have my own car.

That evening I rhapsodized about my new apartment, and my parents both seemed as pleased as I was, though my teenage sister, Connie, showed her ambivalence by rolling her eyes, partly I think, from jealousy. At any rate, it was decided that I would move on Saturday, taking with me my bed, all my books (over four hundred of them) , a night table, one lamp, and a folding chair. Mom would also pack a few dishes, a little bit of silverware, and some linens.

It took almost no time for Dad and me to get my few pathetic things into my apartment. After he left, I built with books a long structure that was shaped like a sofa, stacking more books on either end to suggest sofa arms. Then I covered the whole thing with a Buchanan plaid throw Mom had given me. It actually looked just like a sofa, but the ruse ended the moment people sat down, as if they had just found repose on a stack of bricks. It didn't matter. No relatively more luxurious place I've ever lived has ever given me as glorious a feeling as that first apartment, nor given me such a huge sense of freedom. It provided me the strength to face faculty meetings, Johnny Madison's parents, stacks of papers, which I graded while sitting in bed near the only lamp I had, and the awful corn dog lunches in the teachers' cafeteria.

Chapter 9 Matters of Conscience

Monday came, and nothing about Johnny's behavior or attitude about homework was any different from what it had been in previous weeks. After school I headed for the Madison house, wanting to conclude my visit before Johnny's return from swimming practice. The house was a yellow brick bungalow from the 1920's with trimmed boxwood hedges beneath the picture window. It seemed a perfect example of Norman Rockwell Americana, quite different from the dangerous slum I had expected with its roaming packs of rabid dogs and children.

Mr. Madison, a tall, stately man with silvered temples and wearing a dark suit, answered the front door, inviting me in to sit at the dining room table. I was encouraged by the stacks of books, newspapers and magazines scattered about the living room. It was a house in which a lot of reading occurred on a regular basis. On the side board near where I was sitting, was what I recognized as Johnny's ADVENTURES IN LITERATURE book. The fact that he had even brought it home gave me a glimmer of hope. Of course, he could have brought it home purely to pacify his parents with the ruse that he was really doing his homework. It was an old trick my brother had always used with an algebra book as a prop for making our parents believe he was actually engaged in study, but I dismissed that possibility for Johnny, still believing a glorious transformation of his attitude about school was about to happen.

Mr. Madison had made a pot of tea, which he placed on the table with cups, and a small plate of shortbread cookies. He sat across the table from me and while pouring tea said that he was glad that I had shown an interest in helping his son to succeed in my English class. He then told me that the previous two years for his family had been very difficult, since the drowning death of Johnny's younger sister Sharon. The accident had happened at the summer cottage of friends at Hudson Lake. Afterward, Mrs. Madison went into a state of shock that turned to deep depression from which she was still trying to recover. Johnny too had shut down emotionally, somehow making it through middle school but more and more in need of psychiatric care. He had, the summer before, attempted suicide by hanging himself with a belt in the basement. The school had been notified of these events by the family doctor, but I had been told nothing.

I felt almost speechless at hearing all this news. While I was still processing what Mr. Madison had just told me, my eyes wandered around the room to see water colors and oil paintings signed by Johnny, all of which were nature-scapes with blue lakes. I closed my eyes and caught my breath before thanking Mr. Madison for making clearer to me Johnny's situation and emotional state.

Before I left, Mrs. Madison entered the room. Her husband introduced us, and it was immediately evident by the woman's appearance that her emotional state was fragile. Though probably only in her forties, she already had the worn look of someone much older in her expressionless eyes, disheveled clothing, and in the disinterested shuffle of her walk. She didn't speak but offered her hand and a half-smile that looked as though she had just bought it on sale at Walgreen's. Remembering my attempt to communicate with her by phone, I felt a sudden wave of pity for this woman, still suffering the senseless loss of a daughter and now the slow melting away of her son too. My heart went out to Mr. Madison, who seemed to be the only one holding things together in the family. He shook my hand and then put his arm sympathetically around his wife. The backdrop of Johnny's paintings and his parents standing there looking sad and frail made me remember that I wanted to leave before Johnny's return from swimming practice.

On my walk home I was thinking about the lesson I had just learned painfully, a lesson that would leave its mark on me all the years I taught, that everyone has a story to tell, even if he doesn't tell it in words, and that every life has unhappy circumstances that, if grave enough, can immobilize one's will even to go on living. I saw hope, however, in Johnny's art work, and in the fact that he was at swimming practice. There had to be some kind of motivation in that.

After leaving under mysterious circumstances almost half way through the school year, our speech and debate coach, Miss Pratt, was replaced by Ms. Cora Banks, a woman of reputedly high qualifications, who had taken one of her previous debate teams to Washington for nationals, and whose reputation as a tough task master had preceded her through articles in local newspapers. I met her after Thanksgiving, and we had a Saturday lunch together to discuss upcoming speech and debate meets, as I was to be her assistant in coaching students and going with them and Ms. Banks on the bus to competitions, not only at other high schools in Hammond, but to meets in other cities, like Chesterton, and as far away as Purdue University in Lafayette, Indiana, a good two-hour trip from Hammond. I was paid ten dollars an hour for the extra time after school, including Saturdays, which would help me soon to purchase a car.

Preparation for debates and speech meets was arduous, requiring time after school almost daily. The debate topic for the entire nation in 1969 was "Resolved: that the United States should establish a system of compulsory service by all citizens." Providing proof, refutation, and rebuttal, all carefully timed, required practice. Highly organized and formal, debate before tough and experienced judges made winning its own reward. The topic for the spring of 1970 was, "Resolved: that congress should prohibit unilateral United States military intervention in foreign countries." Even kids who weren't on the debate team were interested in that topic. It struck a timely chord that would have reverberations.

The spring of 1970, when weather became warmer, I was surprised by a school "walk-out," organized by some of the seniors to protest our country's presence in Viet Nam. My sophomores were in on the protest and simply marched out of my classroom at exactly 10:10, leaving the building to congregate in the front parking lot, where there were hundreds of other students, mostly upperclassmen, huddled together, some with posters they had created with messages like, "STOP THE KILLING NOW!" and "WHY A WAR WE CAN'T WIN?" It was obvious that the older students who had organized the walk-out were deadly serious about their message, even though some younger ones saw the whole thing as a temporary escape from class. For some, the satisfaction came probably from the chance to thumb their noses at authority in general.

In fact, my sympathies were with the organizers, many of whom had suffered losses in their own families to a war that no one seemed to understand. The coming incident at Kent State would only increase the horror of the conflict, bringing it home for everyone to witness on TV sets in their own living rooms.

I refused to write up or punish any of my students, who had participated in the protest. Many were thinking about the consequences of slaughter far away, even if not about the immediate results of their defying school rules by leaving class without permission. As someone not much older than they, I was moved by those among them, who were standing up for what they believed. The result was that I was called to the office of Mr. Perkins, who had apparently seen me earlier in the parking lot through the windows of an office he so rarely left.

Mr. Perkins reprimanded me for not hauling my students back into the building. He asked me if I had turned in the names of protesters, and when I said that I had not, he scowled before delivering what sounded like a canned lecture on patriotism and the importance of authority, as well as the danger of encouraging kids to get away with defiant acts against the school, which would, according to him, set a precedent that could eventually unhinge the "entire system." He asked me then if I didn't think that my permissive and dangerous response to the situation shouldn't go on my first-year record as a teacher.

My answer was that first I wanted to go back to his statement about the "entire system." I asked him what that system was and in what way he thought it was being threatened by me or by the students. When he said that teenagers were too young to judge the meaning of a war declared by their country, I almost lost my temper, but I bit my tongue before replying that age had little to do with matters of life and death that had already touched the lives of many of our students, and that many more might soon be placed on the grand conveyor belt to be killed in Asia. I said that I thought that alone gave them the right and perhaps even responsibility to question the "system."

Despite Mr. Perkins's obvious displeasure, I told him that I believed that part of my job as a teacher was to help my students think and make decisions on their own, based upon as much information as they could gather, and that my teaching literature based upon former protesters, like Jonathan Swift, Charles Dickens, and George Orwell, among others, would seem a bit two-faced. I ended my defense (diatribe) by saying that it was more American to stand up peacefully for one's beliefs than to sit passively by, while abstract powers assaulted one's dignity and rights. At that point, Mr. Perkins's fingers on one hand touched the tips of fingers on the other hand, forming the same "cage" in front of his face that he had made at our first meeting the previous August. He said nothing more, except, "Thank you, Mr. Bolinger" and gave me a stare that let me know I was dismissed, at least from his office. Nothing further was ever said on the matter, and no criticism of my "inaction" was ever written on my record. It gave me hope for America.

During my walk to school the next morning, something happened that seemed an omen pointing to the rest of that week. Carrying my leather folder and my thermos of coffee, I passed a filling station, where an expensive-looking red Corvette convertible was just pulling away from the pump. The driver appeared to be around my age, and in his attempt to show off the power of his car, he revved the engine, screeching his tires, and pulling out right in front of me at a speed that made him lose control and crash directly into a telephone pole across the street. Two other cars stopped, the drivers getting out and running with me to see if the speedster was all right. His nose was bleeding from his head probably having hit the steering wheel, but he seemed otherwise to be in good condition, though the front of his car was shaped like the letter "M" from the telephone pole's impact in the center of the hood. One of the other drivers ran back to the station to call the police, as crowds of kids on their way to school were gathering to assess damage for the stories they would undoubtedly be telling in the cafeteria at lunch that afternoon. I continued on my way to school, still believing that because I had been the only one around, the stunt had been for my benefit in order to show how "cool" the stupid driver was. I'll never really know.

Ms. Cora Banks, the new speech teacher and debate coach had been phoning me almost every evening to unload her considerable pack of troubles. She lived with her mother, who owned eighty-some canaries, distributed in cages throughout her home, which over the phone sounded like a huge aviary in some zoo. I also heard the clink of ice cubes in a glass followed nightly by the gradual slurring of Cora's speech. Sometimes I would go about other tasks, grading papers, doing dishes, or writing letters while the phone receiver lay on the night table. Every few minutes I would pick up the phone again to say, "Yes, I know," or "Absolutely!" There were times I even napped, but nothing seemed to make any difference, as there was never any real exchange through actual conversation, because it was never my opinion or advice she sought. She needed only a passive receptacle in which to pour her many sorrows. That container was me. At school I began to notice a change in her behavior too. She seemed disoriented at times, which I thought might be due once again to her nitwit of a boy friend, Lance, not appreciating her.

By Friday of that week, Cora wasn't even in school. She had a substitute teacher, but the faculty buzz was that Cora had not been to her third period class and was later found, sprawled out on a sofa in the faculty lounge, her dress in enough disarray to show a Cinemascopic view of her panties. She had been, according to all accounts I heard, snoring as well, and on the floor next to the sofa, there was a thermos containing only the final remnant of a big, fat Bourbon Old Fashioned. The following Monday, her permanent replacement, Mr. William Farnsworth, was in her old classroom, but that didn't mean that the faculty soap opera was over. Not by a long shot. In any case, I never heard from Cora again.

Chapter 10 Wonders Never Ceasing

Something I learned early in my career as a teacher was not to depend upon the attendance office entirely for making sure students were in class. If a student was absent, I wrote his or her name on the pink attendance slip for that period, the slip then being picked up and taken to the office downstairs, where phone calls were already to have been made by parents first thing that morning to validate those absences. Upon returning to school, students were to go to the attendance office with parental notes even before going to homeroom. The weak links in this laborious and often ineffective system opened the doors of possibility to every Ferris Bueller enrolled at MHS, and there were many. There were students who spent more time and energy coaching each other to imitate parent voices and signatures than in doing homework, and the poor ladies in the attendance office were overworked as it was, trying to deal with more subterfuge than there ever was from the KGB in the Soviet Union.

If there was a questionable absence from my class by a student about whom there was any doubt, I would phone his house myself that evening, and if I wasn't certain it was the parent or guardian I was talking to, I would pay a visit to the home the following day. The reader can well imagine that a visit was not necessary in every case, because word spread quickly about the sinister danger of my method.

The first recipient of a home visit from me was Deirdre Keaton from my second period. She had been absent from my class two Tuesdays in a row, having then brought the required parental note to the attendance office upon her return to school. The third Tuesday she was gone from my class, I called her home for a very enlightening chat with her mother, Mrs. Keaton, who told me she had been completely unaware of any absences by her daughter, but that Deirdre didn't arrive home until after five three afternoons a week due to her being on the girls' tennis team. The Wednesday that I phoned was one of those days when Deirdre would arrive home later, so I asked if I could go to the Keaton house and be there when she got home. Mrs. Keaton loved the idea and said she would put on a pot of coffee. Our visit after school provided a goldmine of information for both Mrs. K and me. I had already talked to the girls' tennis coach, who said that Deirdre had tried out for the team but hadn't made the cut. This meant that three days a week Deirdre was doing something else, and that she had been going somewhere other than my class on three Tuesday mornings.

Mrs. Keaton said that Deirdre liked my class but that she was going through an especially rebellious time, defying both her parents whenever possible. Just after five, Deirdre walked in, placing her tennis racket on a chair by the back door, then removing her coat, which she dropped on the floor after seeing me sitting at the kitchen table holding a coffee mug and smiling. The look of utter shock on her face was to be seen again and again on the faces of other truant students whose homes I would be visiting without warning. Every parent was more than happy to team up with me to get his or her child back on track, or at least back in school. As I said, word spread about my way of dealing with anyone who ditched my class. Imagine a teacher coming to your house. Could there be anything more horrible for someone who's been lying about being in school? Needless to say, the advice, "Don't ditch Mr. B's class. He'll come to your house!" eliminated the problem of truancy for my classes, though it didn't really erase other problems.

There remained unpleasant surprises that sometimes made me wonder if there might be a less agitating profession, like coal mining, research inside volcanoes, or perhaps milking Indian Cobras. One example of my complete dismay in a school situation occurred one afternoon after my lunch supervision, just as I was congratulating myself again on using the microphone to dismiss students by tables that had been cleared of trays or debris.

Deciding to take a little walk with my coffee in hand before my next class, I wandered by the large auditorium, where I noticed a stray pair of gym shoes on the stairs half way up to the balcony. Walking up those stairs, I found the doors, which were usually locked unless there was a program or assembly, ajar, so I went in, moving very slowly in the dimly lit space high above the other 1500 seats on the floor below. Hearing heavy breathing and some high-pitched giggling, I came upon a football jersey draped over one of the folding seats and then a cheerleader's uniform over another seat. On the floor between two rows of the seats were a naked senior boy and girl engaged in what can be described only as an amorous activity with more motion than pistons in a V-8 engine. For a moment they didn't even see me, and I was at first too stunned to say anything, but when I was able to form words, the only ones I could coax from my mouth were, "Do you two have hall passes?" The girl grabbed her sweater to cover her breasts in a gesture that had come laughably late. The boy covered his own equipment with his jersey. I told them to get dressed and meet me downstairs. From there, we went together silently to Mr. Powers's office, where he was sitting behind a cloud of cigar smoke. I told the two that I could relay their story for them, or they could do it themselves. Relieved at their choice to tell their own version of the misadventure, I sat down and remained completely quiet. There was nothing in the disciplinary handbook about fornicating in the balcony, but Mr. Powers stiffened their sentence to three days out of school suspension for not having hall passes while being out of the lunch room. I never saw how Mr. Powers had described in writing the crimes of the two libertines.

The whole experience made me feel, in only one day, like a seasoned veteran, and I decided that this was a story I wouldn't really be able to tell comfortably at dinner parties or in most mixed groups. Had my grandparents asked me, "So, John, What happened in school today?" that story wouldn't be the one I'd be telling them, considering that the worst thing that ever happened in their high school was a girl's pigtail being dipped into the ink well of the desk behind her.

When Deirdre appeared in my class the next morning, Frank, a kid who could gum up any epigram or quotation, looked at her and said, "Wow! Do my eyes beseech me? Are you really back?" There was a hum of muffled talk in the room that made me realize the word was out about my visit to the Keaton home, and that this particular jig was up for Deirdre. After that, there was a notable elevation of respect I received from that class, or maybe it was just terror at the mere thought that I would ever appear at any of their doorsteps too.

My freshmen were reading over a period of four weeks the book ALL CREATURES GREAT AND SMALL by James Herriot, and I showed a 16 mm film version of the episode about Mrs. Pumphrey and her spoiled Pekinese, Tricky-Woo. I had classes write narratives on their own stories about pets and was pleasantly surprised by the stories of love and devotion so many had experienced for their dogs, cats, turtles, and even a lizard named Clarence. We did a large bulletin board, tacking up narratives, photographs, drawings, and a painting of memories of their pets. It was really very touching, and though I invited the principal, Mr. Perkins, to see the display, he never ventured upstairs to see it. In fact, one afternoon in May, when temperatures on the second floor were warm enough to cure beef jerky, Mr. Perkins did pop his head briefly into my classroom just long enough to look at the thermostat registering 87 and to say, "Carry on." After he left, one of my freshmen raised his hand to ask, "Who was that guy?" My response said everything any of my students would ever need to know about the "stranger." "That was Mr. Perkins, the principal of our school." Then a puzzled look spread across the faces of most in the room, as though they had just been let in on a dark secret that had been successfully kept from them for the previous eight months.

My apartment was taking shape in the used furniture I had purchased to make it feel more like a real home, a chest of drawers, three lamps, a chair for the bedroom, a kitchen table with four chairs, a desk, and one brand new piece, a large leather wing chair for which I paid a staggering $300, but which I still have forty-three years later.

The final test for this place becoming my real home was to have guests over for dinner. My only experiences as a chef had been in college while sharing an off campus Victorian house with eight other guys, who all had duties to keep the place running, like doing laundry, washing dishes, cleaning rooms, vacuuming, trash removal, grocery shopping, and of course, cooking, which was my province, or at least they thought it was. It should be added here that not one of us could ever have been called anything remotely close to a gourmet. It's really a wonder to me that no one in the house died eating my cooking. They would eat anything that didn't eat them first, including an old tennis shoe, as long as it was cooked long enough and flavored with something like thousand island dressing. My challenge then for this dinner party in my own apartment was to come up with a guest list and a menu, as long as the invitees didn't exceed three, as I had only four dining chairs.

My guests would be two teachers from the English Department, Miss Mason, the chair, and Logan Clark, a veteran teacher of two years, one of those having been spent as an instructor in Hawaii, and who would become chair of the English Department for sixteen years. I had to do my best for the two most important people in my department, people who had been kind and had mentored me.

My grandmother, who had a spectacular garden, brought two lovely bouquets of roses and tulips to me, along with four place settings of her best Havilland china with wine and water stemware, and silver. She also brought a cream colored damask tablecloth with napkins and silver candle holders. I can still see Grandpa carrying those boxes up the stairs to my apartment, his Dr. Grabow pipe puffing like a tiny chimney and leaving the aroma of his mellow tobacco in the hallway.

I prepared the food myself from carefully considered recipes, and the menu included dill and cucumber canapes, curried pumpkin soup, roasted chicken breast in cream sauce, green salad with walnuts and lemon vinaigrette, and ice cream with oatmeal raisin cookies. The wine was red Bordeaux. Aside from the chicken being a bit overcooked, the dinner went very well. We had our coffee in the living room, where I had made sure there were three other chairs so that no one had to sit on the hard sofa made of books. The radio played classical music on WFMT, and conversation flowed easily, as it generally does among teachers of English. Winifred and Logan were appreciative guests and seemed to have enjoyed the evening, not leaving until after eleven, which I saw as a good sign. After cleaning up, I looked around my little apartment, happy at having entertained my first guests.

My energy was still too high for me to sleep, so I decided to take out the stacks of the latest essay I had assigned my freshmen. I took first the ones from period six, leafing through them quickly to see if Johnny Madison had even turned in a paper. He had, and there was a note paper-clipped to the essay, which asked that none of what he had written be read aloud or shared in any way with anyone, because it was so "private," a word he had underlined. The assignment had been to write two pages about something or someone that had had changed their lives, perhaps in a personal way, forever. Johnny's title was simply, "Sharon." The content expressed his guilt at not being a good enough swimmer to save his little sister from drowning two years before, even though in other ways he had always been her protector. The idea that he had failed her continued to haunt him and had created in him a rage, "like molten lava," that he couldn't always control. He was angry at himself and at the world.

By the time I finished reading those two pages, the front of my shirt was wet in spots from the first tears I had shed since my dog Sleepy had died fifteen years before.

Chapter 11 Freshmen Fake Book Reports and Other Foibles

When I was a student in high school, girls had carried around tattered old copies of books like GONE WITH THE WIND, and PEYTON PLACE. During my first year of teaching, more than half of the girls in the school carried, among their other books, copies of Erich Segal's wildly, if mysteriously, popular LOVE STORY, a sentimental Romeo and Juliet kind of tragedy of surprising brevity, that became a best seller and stayed on the charts for way too long. I read it myself just so that I could discuss it intelligently, if not enthusiastically, with the girls in my classes. Reading tastes for boys had not changed much since my days in high school. MAD MAGAZINE was still at the top of their list of "cool" reading material with CRACKED coming in a close second. These were tough competition for the selections I was assigning my freshmen, books like, GREAT EXPECTATIONS, 1984, ROBINSON CRUSOE, THE GRAPES OF WRATH, THE OLD MAN AND THE SEA, JUNGLE BOOK, THE PEARL, ALL CREATURES GREAT AND SMALL, TREASURE ISLAND, THE PRINCE AND THE PAUPER, LITTLE WOMEN, and NIGHT (Weisel). Students also had to read at least two other books of their own choice, submitting written reports on them by the end of the term.

To get my freshmen thinking about those extra book possibilities, I compiled a list of titles, most of which had not been made into films, with brief summaries of the stories. Two of those titles and summaries I fabricated completely, curious to see if anyone might try to do a report on a book that didn't even exist. Freshmen are experts at creating more baloney than Alaska creates snow, so it was a matter of interest to see what might happen. FIRST BASE, SECOND BASE I said was about a boy named Carl from the slums of New York's lower East Side, who became a great player for the Yankees, despite grinding poverty and childhood illness. The other phony book was ROSES AND THORNS, the story of an Irish girl named Fiona, who rose from foster care to become, with her husband's help, a great nurse and advocate of child care. I added the comment that I had not read those two particular books.

Two boys turned in reports on FIRST BASE, SECOND BASE, padded with the most creative but ridiculous rubbish. Three girls submitted their reports on ROSES AND THORNS, providing even more extraneous nonsense than the boys had been able to invent, including some silly stuff about the author. All this showed me that students could become great opportunists when given the chance, especially if it meant not having to do a lot of extra work. It was also a mirror image of what I had been as a high school freshman. It made me begin to think that maybe sneaky people could make decent teachers for high school kids.

Debbie Brown, who had already plagiarized Elizabeth Barrett Browning's most famous poem, asked me one afternoon if she could do a report on a book called CANDY, and thinking she had said CANDIDE, I gave her the OK. At the time, I thought that Voltaire's satire might be a bit much for Debbie to digest, but it was a relatively short book, so I thought that if she had any problems with it, she could come to me for help. I thought no more about it until a week later, when she turned in her written report on CANDY, a piece of embarrassingly vile pornography about a prostitute, the namesake of the novel. In her paper Debbie revealed details that would make a sailor blush and that made me begin to worry that if her parents found out that I had approved such a piece of trash as reading material for a freshman (or anyone else), I could soon expect a message over the P.A. saying, "Will Mr. Bolinger report to the main office. Please clean out your desk first." As it turned out, I graded the report, adding a note that I had misunderstood the title she had originally given to me. Nothing further was ever said about it, but I continued to imagine a book with a partially clad prostitute on the cover at the Brown house, placed tastefully on a coffee table next to copies of BETTER HOMES AND GARDENS.

I encouraged all my students to read, wanting them to enjoy reading as much as I did. Also, I tried to promote the school's amazing theatrical productions by giving extra credit to those who tried out for productions and were chosen, or who helped out by being on stage crew. In high school I had been in only one play, a very weak production of OUR TOWN that would have made Thornton Wilder commit suicide right there in the theater. I played the drunk church organist in Grover's Corners. The only other play I remember my high school producing was HILLBILLY WEDDIN'. By amazing contrast, Morton High School, where I was a teacher, did massive and high quality productions of musicals like, CARNIVAL, CAROUSEL, OLIVER, and OKLAHOMA. Other plays were done equally well like, ARSENIC AND OLD LACE, and even ROMEO AND JULIET. Those shows always made me feel proud to be a teacher in that school.

The choral department had standards just as high and did concerts at Christmas and in the spring yearly, that would have impressed the most discerning tastes. I never missed a concert or play all the years I taught at MHS and always had goose bumps while sitting in the audience watching especially those kids I thought would surely end up on AMERICA'S MOST WANTED list. Being at those performances gave me a deeper perspective on what our students could do and how important something could be to them. This of course included their performances on basketball courts, wrestling mats, soccer, baseball, football fields, and at swim meets. It meant so much to them that their parents and teachers were there to cheer them on, even if they didn't always say so.

A conflict arose between me and a Baptist minister in the community, whose flock included a girl named Roberta in my third period English I class. At the time, my freshmen were reading ROMEO & JULIET, a play filled with some of the most glowing and sumptuous poetry in our language. In class we did readings, sometimes making audio tape recordings of scenes that included battle sound effects with cafeteria butter knives as swords. Those were the scenes the boys seemed to enjoy most, but girls appreciated the figurative language, and the innocence of the two lovers, something already familiar to some of those girls. Maureen Eason, for example, sat in the back of the room weeping over some of the lines from the first balcony scene, when Juliet was testing Romeo's sincerity at his swearing his love for her by the moon, "That tips with silver all these fruit-tree tops" and Juliet's response, "Oh swear not by the moon, the inconstant moon, that monthly changes in her circled orb, lest that thy love prove likewise variable." Then when Romeo asks what he should swear by, Juliet answers, "Do not swear at all, or if thou wilt, swear by thy gracious self, which is the god of my idolatry." There was little Maureen in the back row, shedding tears over those lines. Many more tears came from other girls at the play's sad conclusion, tears I would never have expected from freshmen.

In front of me right now is an old copy of the text we used that spring of 1970. Signatures, in the inside cover, of students who used the book over the years are still in the "rented to" column next to signatures of teachers, several of whom have since died, who used the same book in their freshman English classes. The names Norman, Dana, Brenda, Jeff, Pam, Bobby, Lisa, Gretchen, and Robert are still there, a roster of some of those who held the book in their hands, some loving it, some hating it, some reading it just to get by. I don't know why, but I feel as moved seeing that little history in those signatures on that page as I ever was by the play itself. I suppose it's a little like looking at an old family album and remembering good things again.

Half way through our study of that play in the spring of that year, I received an official-looking letter from Pastor Jeffry Bowman of the First Baptist Church. The communication was an admonition against my teaching the play, ROMEO & JULIET. The pastor had heard from some of his parishioners that the play was being taught. His contention was that his church did not believe in or condone "sexual intercourse before marriage." My first thought was that there must be another play called ROMEO & JULIET about which I knew nothing. All my attempts to contact Pastor Bowman by telephone having been thwarted by his secretary, I finally wrote a letter to say that the play about which he had written in his letter was definitely not the play we were reading in class and that ours was the one by William Shakespeare, in which there was no "sex before marriage," except an innocently affectionate kiss in the balcony scene. I never heard back from him on the subject.

Weeks later, however, I received another letter from Pastor Bowman, again criticizing my choice of literature, this time for my sophomore English class, which was then reading 2001 A SPACE ODYSSEY by Arthur C. Clarke, a book in which the pastor claimed man's evolution from apes was being taught. My letters of reassurance that evolution was not being taught at all never received a response. It was later learned that the pastor had also, without reason, been grandstanding from his pulpit about his righteous diatribe against "the sinful teachings in our public schools." I also found out that another English teacher had received a letter from the same pastor, criticizing her teaching of Emily Bronte's WUTHERING HEIGHTS, another to a teacher using Mark Twain's PUDDINHEAD WILSON, and to a biology teacher for even using the word "evolve" in his classroom lectures.

Had Pastor Bowman not been an absolute buffoon, we teachers might have felt intellectually bullied or educationally terrorized, but in order for his threats to have carried any weight, the "bully" in question would have needed to possess intellect or education, both of which were utterly absent from his list of alleged virtues.

Despite these minor verbal scuffles, teaching went on its way with the support of almost all parents and cooperative efforts of most students. Johnny Madison's father had a long talk with him on the subject of the love he and his wife had for their son. The talk evidently included some reference to the genuine concern of his English teacher. Whatever was said in that talk seemed to have a positive effect on Johnny's work in my class, not all at once, but gradually over the rest of that term. Even though he had failed English I and would have to take it again in summer school, Johnny would be receiving a credit for English II and become one of my most capable writers. Another triumph of second semester was that though Debbie Brown's poems continued to be the most awful tripe I had ever read, there was no more plagiarism. That poetry was absolutely hers!

Chapter 12 Confessions of a Public School Teacher

I heard once in an old movie, starring Monty Woolley, that even on your deathbed you shouldn't make any confessions until you feel the rigor mortis setting in, because you might otherwise just recover and then live with miserable regret for years to come. I'm going to take the chance though of making a confession that perhaps many other teachers wouldn't.

If school teachers are completely honest (and I'm not sure that anyone can be "completely" honest), they will admit that the challenge of inspiring and motivating their students can sometimes become more difficult due just to one or two in the class, whose neediness or orneriness becomes the prime source for disruption of whatever focus was planned for the day's lesson. As a first-year teacher, you may on occasion find the placid surface of your yet persistent senior-year, college ideals churned up by the speedboat maneuvers of a student, who is hungry for attention, power, or just plain revenge for an educational system he has hated since kindergarten. In what I hope are only the rarest cases, you may encounter a kid for whom all of the above is applicable. In such an instance, if you can socialize the student by tapping his inner gifts, you should be eligible for a Nobel Prize; if not, the whole community should pitch in to purchase for his parents a gift certificate to the nearest exorcist.

I find it interesting (a courteous word for strange) that nothing in college methods classes seems even to address the possibility that one day there may actually be a socially or mentally disturbed student enrolled in your class. That bright, sun-shiny world of methods classes doesn't really want to talk about such a contingency that might mess up any happy statistics on a teacher doing such and such a thing to produce such and such a result. Demonic behavior in a child is almost too disturbing to discuss in a society where shifting the blame to parents, teachers, or to society itself is so much more sanitary. That's why addressing social difficulties while one is still young is so very important, not just to render society safer, but also to rehabilitate those who may not be able to function in "civilized" ways. Fortunately, it's the rarest challenge we as educators have, but that doesn't make it any less momentous a task and responsibility.

I'm not sure the term "social misfit" is even used anymore, but if it is, it has to be only as a last resort. Education is designed, I hope, to help people function better in a world, where they can be productive without endangering or impeding the progress of others. We sometimes forget that in a room with thirty students, twenty-nine are often, for practical purposes, brushed aside in favor of the teacher's having to deal most of the time with the thirtieth child, who is disruptive, for whatever reason. I suppose that most of the worst and most dangerous sociopaths were ones who simply slipped through the cracks in public schools.

In fact, there were over the years only a very few students from my classes, who ended up in juvenile hall and then prison, none being there for life or wanted for murder. Wonderful, isn't it? In that respect, maybe I have nothing about which to complain. I did, however, have in my classes from time to time students who were just annoying in what appeared occasionally to have become a sacred mission on their parts. All public school teachers of middle or high school kids must deal with those.

Even from the beginning of my years as a teacher, I didn't send students to the office or to sit in the hallway. Dumping the responsibility of discipline on somebody else never made sense to me. I figured if I couldn't make a difference myself by re-channeling a kid's anger or mischief, I wasn't worth much as a teacher. Besides, I didn't want misbehavior to become a ticket out of class, even if it meant a trip down to the Hades of Mr. Powers's office, that horrible underworld, where there was often loud yelling, followed by weeping into a ply from that famous box of Heather Breeze Tissues with the ballerina on the box. No, handling problems myself made more sense.

Classroom rules revolve always around mutual respect. The golden rule is of prime importance, and almost every behavior precept comes from it. I discovered over time that positive reinforcement and rewards, like writing a wonderful letter of praise home to surprised parents worked wonders, when a usually cantankerous kid did something positive in my class. Taking a student into the hall for a brief one-to-one talk (talking and listening) is so much more valuable than scolding and embarrassing him in front of peers, which often only increases the level of attention he craves anyway. Education isn't about control. I found more and more that treating students more like adults yielded from them more grown-up behavior. Listening to their concerns, when they were willing to share them, and tuning in to their angst and to why there were negative feelings almost always made a difference, even if not the first time. Your pupils know when you care and when you care enough not to give up on them. You will be tested sometimes over many weeks.

It's usually not even because of a teacher's class, but rather because there are outside conflicts and circumstances that a student chooses to make the teacher his whipping post. Listening to students and reading what they write can help them believe in your concern, your belief in their abilities, and your sincere desire that they succeed. Most of classroom behavior goes back to those precepts.

A good friend of mine, who was also in the English Department and a splendidly capable and dedicated teacher was distraught one day, because a mean-spirited boy had glued a Webster's Dictionary to the floor in her classroom, necessitating a janitor's removing the tiles in the area and replacing them. To anyone not in charge of a classroom, that incident may actually sound comical, but it wasn't funny to my friend, who pondered painfully why anyone would have done such a thing.

I'm afraid I have a strong vein of sarcasm winding through me, which I have to work hard to keep under control. In attempting to cope with the rigors of teaching that tiny minority of ill-behaved students, I found it occasionally helpful to write what was really on my mind....after I sent the genuine letters to parents. I think teachers will appreciate the following example, which I ran across recently and wrote in December of 1995, and which was particularly satisfying. I recommend it as a way to release tension without having to kill any of the kids. I have, of course, changed the names.

December 8, 1995
Morton High School
6915 Grand Ave.
Hammond, Indiana 46323

Dear Mrs. Patrick,

Having made every effort to instruct your son Leland Patrick for the past two years in the subject of English and having tried to teach him the rudiments of civilized behavior in a world that will undoubtedly reduce him to the status of a street person, I have come to the unalterable conclusion that your son will have to be put to sleep.

This may come as something of a shock to you and perhaps seem rather politically incorrect, but given the history of Leland's behavior and prospects for his improvement, you will probably agree that this solution is the most humane for everyone concerned. It makes much more sense financially, as Leland's chances of any kind of employment are somewhat slimmer than those of Ralph Nader being elected President of The United States or Jay Leno receiving the Nobel Prize for physics. The needle on the school Irritation Meter has flown off the machine several times when Leland was in the same room, and blood pressure for any living creature reaches dangerous levels in proximity to Leland's annoying banter.

Let me assure you that the Morton faculty will make this as convenient for you as possible. The procedure will not even have to be done in your home but can be done in the counselor's office downstairs (lethal injection). There is even a cremation facility in the school's boiler room. Leland's ashes can be mailed to you in a tastefully appointed little box, cunningly decorated with all of Leland's old conduct grades in gilded letters. We want to be as accommodating as possible, which is why our original plans of tying your son to the railroad tracks between Kennedy Avenue and Indianapolis Boulevard have been abandoned due to the inevitable mess and bad publicity for your family.

In conclusion, let me encourage you to take advantage of this splendid offer while it lasts. Other unhappy parents are waiting in line to engage our services in this most discreet solution. In your case it is surely the answer to a question that has plagued us for all the years that your son has been a sophomore at Morton High School. My only other comment, though it comes too late, is that you should have danced all night. God bless you.

Sincerely,

John Bolinger

This private manner of using a written steam valve to release tension was one that worked quite well for me. One drawer of my desk was for the letters I really sent to parents, and another drawer was for the letters I would never actually send. The result was that in my classroom the milk of human kindness flowed much more abundantly than it could have, had there been no safe way for me to get rid of my frustration. Thank God I never mailed letters from the wrong drawer!

Chapter 13 Summer Respite

My first year of teaching had not been the trial by fire it might have been, though I still had so much to learn. After final exams were taken, all the students left for the summer, and I sat at my school desk, which was covered with test papers and grade sheets for each class. Because there were no computers for classroom use in 1970, records of attendance along with final grades, had to be entered by hand in pencil on scan sheets, a process that with grading all those papers could take many hours. I can't think of another profession for which after-hours work is so unrelenting. There, my whining is out of the way now. There I sat as I would at the close of seventy semesters over the coming years, using up no fewer than 1200 red pens, that would bleed over students' papers until the summer of 2004. I knew, though, that I was in the right place, doing what I did best. Debbie Brown, Deirdre Keaton, and Johnny Madison had been my greatest challenges that first year, but I was proud of their progress and knew that they were going to be all right.

The French teacher, Mrs. Graham, was planning to retire after one more year, so the powers that be decided that I would be given a beginning French class. Presumably, Mrs. Graham would be able to monitor my teaching during her final year before handing over her little French empire of classes to me, not gift-wrapped, but with the understanding that I pay my dues by taking a first-year class to prove my mettle. That was enough to inspire me to begin graduate work that summer by enrolling in Temple University's summer-abroad program in Paris, France. Buying myself a car would just have to wait.

I had been to Paris before. During my junior year in college I had spent time in Normandy, while my sister studied in Brittany. I was also in Paris that year for a few weeks, but now I would be taking courses in 20th Century French literature and in French composition. Success would yield me several credits toward my master's degree, something the state of Indiana required of its public school teachers within the first five years in its employ.

A few days after school was out, my parents drove me to O'Hare Air Port, for me to catch a flight to London, where I would explore for two or three days before getting a flight to Paris. I still have the plaid wool muffler I bought at Harrods on Brampton Road. My only other memories of my time in London are of Covent Garden, where I saw a performance of Handel's opera, RINALDO, and visits to Kew Gardens, and Chelsea Gardens, otherwise living inexpensively by staying in a hotel room so modest, that it was only one step above a camping tent. The flight to Paris was quiet enough for me to sleep for a while, despite the brevity of the trip.

Arriving at Orly Air Port, I got a cab to the hotel where Professor Rosemary Hodgins of Temple University, Philadelphia would be meeting me and some other Americans to administer some tests for our placement in classes at the university. We took a series of written tests on French grammar and history in a large room with 18th Century paneling and plaster work, a room in which Louis XVI might have felt quite at home. By that evening the scores had been tallied and the results posted on a bulletin board at the same hotel, where we picked up our class schedules along with information on our accommodations at the Sorbonne.

I and my Baltimore roommate, Michael, would share a very pleasant "chambre" with private bath on the second floor of the "Fondation des Etats Unis" with huge French windows overlooking a formal courtyard garden, filled with flowers, statuary, and sets of wrought iron tables and chairs. The Fondation was part of the University of Paris, where I would be taking upper division classes for which Temple University would be giving me six hours of graduate credits, if I succeeded.

Everything at the school was within walking distance, but I took the metro (Parisian subway) to places I had been before and to new places that would become my haunts that summer, especially on the Rive Gauche (Left Bank), where the Sorbonne is nestled, the school founded in 1257 by Robert de Sorbon. The area is still called "Le Quartier Latin" (The Latin Quarter) from the Middle Ages when Latin was spoken there by students, professors, clergy, and everyone else who was "educated." Latin had been, for centuries, the universal language of Europe.

It was exciting to attend lectures in the round chemistry lecture hall, a huge kind of indoor amphitheater with tiered, curved, heavy oak benches more than halfway around the enormous room, with a huge, carved oak desk/lab table, where Madame Pernod lectured about 20th Century French writers, including Albert Camus, Jean Paul Sartre, Simone de Beauvoire, and Jean Anouilh, while she puffed on a cigarette, which was always in a tortoise shell holder. A statuesque woman of striking, dark beauty, Madame Pernod also possessed a stunning speaking voice that made being in her classes an exotic experience.

Adding to this intoxicating experience was the collection of small polished brass plaques scattered about the seating areas where former students, like Victor Hugo, Louis Pasteur, Jean Jacques Rousseau, Voltaire, and the French chemist, Lavoisier had sat listening to lectures too in previous centuries. I was completely filled with awe, even when one morning Madame Pernod, during an enthusiastically sweeping gesture with her cigarette to drive home a point she was making about the writer Andre Gide, fell off the high stool that was generally her perch for those lectures. Even from the highest areas of seating in the room, we could see only a gray curl of smoke rising above her desk, followed by a bejeweled hand grasping the inner edge of the massive desk, pulling her to an upright position from which she continued making her point, as if nothing had happened, before taking another long drag from the cigarette, even though it was then slightly bent.

It was a scene that as a teacher I would never forget over the coming years, when during my talks with classes, the chalk would break, I would trip over myself, or step awkwardly into a wastepaper basket. Going right on, as though unaffected, worked pretty well most of the time, even though students had to work hard sometimes to stifle their laughter whenever classroom work was interrupted by my unintentional slapstick.

The frightening part of classes at the Sorbonne was having to stand occasionally in front of the class and Madame Pernod to expound in French upon aspects of books we were reading, like LA PESTE (THE PLAGUE) and L'ETRANGER (THE STRANGER) by Camus,

NAUSEE (NAUSEA), and LES MAINS SALES (DIRTY HANDS) by Sartre, and LES VOYAGEURS SANS BAGAGES (TRAVELERS WITHOUT LUGGAGE) by Jean Anouilh. After those experiences, I would never again be afraid to speak in front of any other group.

At the Fondation des Etats Unis there were students from all over the world, speaking Chinese, Arabic, Japanese, Swedish, German, Polish, Russian, Spanish, and English, but when we would gather at the tables in little groups in the evenings in the garden to play cards, suddenly the air was filled with varied, accented versions of French, that unifying tongue that brought us all together in a world that often seemed otherwise fragmented. I never again felt so cosmopolitan as I did during those balmy and flower-fragrant, summer evenings, sipping wine, and losing at cards.

Within walking distance of the university was L'Isle de la Cite, that little island, the jewel of which is the Cathedral of Notre Dame of Paris, a building in which even a sneeze sounds beautiful. But my favorite place to visit almost daily was the Musee de Cluny, a monastery built in 1340 near Gallo-Roman thermal baths. Now a museum, the thirty-four rooms of the stone building house perhaps Europe's finest collection of Medieval and Renaissance art, including paintings, tapestries, sculpture in stone and wood, laces, clothing, jewelry, bronze, enamels, ivory, china, and suits of armor. What I loved best was the cool silence of those rooms. There were hardly ever any other visitors, so the caretakers came to know me by name in those serene rooms filled with light filtered through antique stained glass windows, and where anyone would have a spiritual experience. Many tourists overlook this amazing place, perhaps because it is off the beaten path and has neither the fame nor the bustle of other more magnificent museums like the Louvre, which I visited almost daily as well, on the Right Bank.

Michael wasn't very talkative but was much more studious than I and willing to spend most of his evenings in our room, hunched over his books. We did, however, meet a couple of charming girls, one an American named Margaret from New Jersey, also studying at the university for the summer, and Claudine from Dijon. We saw Margaret daily at school, but Claudine was spending a month with her parents at her aunt's home just south of Paris. Both girls were in their early twenties, as were Michael and I. They were entertaining company on our double dates at restaurants and on visits to the dazzling gardens of Montparnasse, Parc Montsouris, Luxembourg Gardens, and Versailles, the former royal palace about an hour from Paris by car or train.

Claudine, who was always my date, was a tall, slender, redhead, of classic beauty like that of women in Pre-Raphaelite paintings. She was a graduate of a university in Lyons and had hopes of practicing law in the suburbs of Paris. We shared a love of music, attending together three performances in just one week of Puccini's LA BOHEME and two of CARMEN by Bizet at the Opera Comique. She, Michael, Margaret, and I attended together performances at the Comedie Francaise of Rostand's CYRANO DE BERGERAC, and Moliere's LE BOURGEOIS GENTILHOMME, and his LE MISANTHROPE. We would all occasionally have lunch together in one of the park gardens, dining simply on a crusty loaf of French bread, some cheese, and fruit with a bottle of inexpensive red wine, the sounds of water splashing in fountains, and birds singing in the many trees. I remember those days fondly and still imagine sometimes what it might be like to live in Paris, with access to all the beauty and cultural exhilaration the City of Lights provides in such abundance. Our "Cartes d'Etudiants" (student ID cards) gave us free entry to almost all exhibitions and museums and cut prices in half for concerts and even meals at some restaurants. It was heaven.

One of the things that impressed me most about my stay in Paris that summer was the deep appreciation for culture shared by all the French whom I met. Street sweepers, executives, waiters, rich and poor alike, showed pride and appreciation for the arts. Time and time again, I would meet French people, who were enraptured by art exhibits everywhere from the Louvre to the Jeu de Paume (which later became the Musee d'Orsay for modern art, including the French Impressionists), at concerts in parks, and in theaters all over the city. One case in particular was an elderly man with his grandchildren. The man was a street worker with rough laborer's hands, doubtless working at minimum wage, who wanted his son's children to be exposed to the grace and charm of CYRANO DE BERGERAC. At the play's conclusion, when Cyrano died, and colored paper leaves fell from stage prop trees, the old man was leaning over the balcony railing in tears, dabbing his eyes with an old handkerchief and telling me that he had always had the same reaction the many times he had already seen the play.

I had been told by many Americans, who had been to Paris several times, to expect rudeness and sarcasm by Parisians, and reminded more than once (by sarcastic Americans) of George Bernard Shaw's dictum that the French don't really care what you say, as long as you pronounce it correctly. Instead, perhaps because I spoke French modestly well, I found the Parisians to be far more patient than I expected, and even kind, despite the frequently oafish behavior of so many American tourists, who seemed to judge everything based upon what they were used to at home.

Another incident I recall clearly happened while Claudine and I were dining at a little restaurant in the Montparnasse area. While we were enjoying our dessert and coffee, a loud, American man entered the place with his wife and children. Without hesitation or any sense of decorum whatsoever, he pointed to the table he wanted, even though there was a "reserved" sign there. The maitre d' told him politely in English that there were no tables left, which prompted the vociferous visitor to pull out his wallet and take out a big wad of francs, that he then waved in the face of the embarrassed maitre d'. Explaining once again that the table was reserved, the maitre d' turned to walk away and go about his business. The American responded by yelling, "This would never happen in Texas, where I'm from. You foreigners are all alike." I'm sure the irony never occurred to the man as he and his family retreated out the door from what might have become a true international incident, had the waiter not been used to such stupidity. All I could think of then was something my dad had said to me when I was younger, "Why don't you try using your head for something besides a hat rack." I pictured the American man we had just seen using his head for no other purpose than to support a ten-gallon chapeau.

An experience that further endeared me to the French involved a trip I took alone by train from Paris to Vaux le Vicomte, a chateau I admired more than the Palace of Versailles. The chateau was built in the 17th Century by Nicolas Fouquet, a minister of finance for Louis XIV, even before Colbert. The chateau of Monsieur Fouquet, along with its magnificent gardens and fountains was the prime inspiration for Versailles, an inspiration that began August 17, 1661, when the king himself was invited to attend perhaps the greatest and most elaborate fete of the century at Fouquet's home. The food, music, fireworks, and tour of the fabulous chateau impressed Louis to the point of jealousy, which then turned to suspicion, and an investigation, including some trumped-up charges by Jean Baptiste Colbert, head minister of finance, of embezzlement on Fouquet's part. How many of those charges were based upon fact has always been in dispute, but shortly after the fete, Monsieur Fouquet was arrested and thrown into prison, where he finally died in 1680. His chateau and all its treasures were seized by the crown, and the same year, Louis began construction of the massive Palais de Versailles, which would continue to drain the French economy, paving a golden path to revolution more than a century later.

But, "Revenons a nos moutons," an old French saying that means, "Let's get back to our sheep" or back to matters at hand. I already mentioned that the trip to Vaux le Viscomte endeared me even more to the French, but I need to explain how that endearment came about.

There was hardly anyone else at the chateau the sunny afternoon in July when I paid my visit. As I wandered through the richly appointed salons, admiring furniture and gilt moldings that reminded me of wedding and birthday cakes, I stopped at a bust of Jean de la Fontaine, the 17th Century writer of fables in the most beautiful and elegant French ever composed. I then heard a man's voice. "Excusez-moi, monsieur." I had dropped my return train ticket on the floor in front of another bust, one of Moliere. Handing me the ticket, he introduced me to his wife and their teenage son and daughter, and we began talking about the chateau, which they had visited many times.

Our conversation expanded to include music, art, theater, sports, and food. Monsieur and Madame Dupres loved Gershwin and American jazz, while their children, Amande and Maurice, liked American rock. As we all walked together through the chateau gardens, it was only after an hour that we all seemed to feel we had known each other for years. The father was an engineer for public works in Paris but he and his family lived not far from the chateau and invited me to have dinner with them at their home before my trip back to Paris. I accepted with great pleasure and cannot even now remember any other dining or conversational experience I've enjoyed more. I learned a lot from Maurice and his sister Amande about the lycee (high school) they attended. Their home was a charming country kind of place with a lovely garden that smelled of lavender.

When it was time for me to head back to Paris, the Dupres family drove me to the station and gave me a bottle of red Bordeaux and a loaf of French bread to take with me back to the dorm, where Michael polished off both by himself. After I returned to America, the Dupres family and I even wrote some letters to each other. It was an amazing connection, which I can never imagine could happen again with any other family. We lost touch over the years, but the last news I had from them was in a New Year's card that Maurice had become a doctor of law and was working in the French tribunal. They will always remain for me the ideal French family, intelligent, warm, outgoing lovers of life.

My final days in Paris that summer were spent preparing for and taking written and oral exams. The written parts I took at the Sorbonne, after which I walked into the main courtyard to put my old, torn trench coat on a statue of Louis Pasteur, encouraged by the applause of other students in the area, as I tied the belt around Pasteur's waist, but also afraid of my picture appearing the next day on the front page of LE MONDE with a story about an American vandal. In any case, I never went back for the coat and have always wondered how long it remained on the statue.

The oral part of exams was unusual in that it was based upon having dinner at a restaurant on the Left Bank with Professor Hodgins and Professor Pernod. Only two students at a time would spend an hour or two with the two "grandes dames" over lunch or dinner, so the oral exams took several days to administer to all students in our class. Michael and I had dinner with the two professors for over two hours one evening at the Trianon Rive Gauche. Conversation meandered through topics of French culture, and what we had learned over the summer. No English, of course! The wine flowed throughout what I consider the most civilized and most thoroughly French exam I ever took. My grades for the written and oral exams were seventeen and eighteen, respectively, on the French scale of twenty, so I was granted my six graduate credits in French toward my master's degree.

I arrived back in Indiana on a warm August afternoon, ready and even anxious to prepare for the start of the coming school year at MHS.

Chapter 14 Back Home in Indiana

Hoosiers are a very particular part of the human species, but perhaps echoed by other parts of our country and the world with not all of which I'm completely familiar. Even more particular are the residents of that northwest part of the state called, for better or worse, "Da Region." An industrial, blue-collar town during most of the years I taught there, it has retained a rough-around-the-edges reputation for hard working, hard drinking, and no-frills attitude based upon memories of The Great Depression and unemployment before the Gary and East Chicago steel mills assured jobs, at least to men, for even those who had no high school diplomas.

"Da Region" includes several communities of Lake County, which remains heavily unionized for the labor force, including school teachers. Friday nights the Blue Bird Tap on Kennedy Avenue in Hammond was always overflowing with regular clientele. My cousin Cathy used to put her head just inside the door to see the crowded, smoke-filled, dark space to yell, "Hey, Dad! Mom wants you to come home right away!" Then retreating to the parking lot, she would double over with laughter at the sudden exit of at least six guys going to their cars to head on home.

If there was any problem at all in teaching French to Northwest Indiana Hoosiers, it was that French was viewed as some kind of luxury, something frilly and totally unnecessary in order to function in a world that was all about paying bills on time, having clothes to wear, and enough to eat. That practical framework of values didn't include knowing any more French than what R.S.V.P. meant, and certainly didn't include the need to know anything at all about "pate de foie gras" or that Coco Chanel wasn't some new kind of kid cereal.

My work was cut out for me, especially my having just returned from Paris, a city that in values and cultural richness was light years from Hammond, Indiana. However, I enjoyed the challenge of trying to win people over to new ways of looking at the world. For me it was what education was about, and it made me feel a little like Marco Polo returning to Italy with exotic stories and knowledge of China, strange and remote as another planet. To Hoosiers, Paris was an alien planet too (as Indiana would have been to Parisians), but that had its advantages in my presenting material that was definitely not more of the same old stuff. The greatest thing on my side, though, was that I genuinely liked Indiana, Morton High School, as well as the parents and students. My family and most of my friends were in the Region too. It was home.

The first day of school that September of 1970, the heat on the second floor was excessive to the point that I loosened my necktie, removed my jacket, and rolled up my shirt sleeves. Students were draped over their desks, like old wet rags by afternoon so that after I had passed out text books and taken roll, I took my sixth period French I class to the shade and relative cool of the inner courtyard garden. I also took with me enrollment cards, because I always had beginning French students write on the backs of those cards why they had chosen French over Spanish or German. I also asked for answers to two other questions, "Where is France?" and "What is the capital of France?" Their answers helped me to establish where we all were at the start of the course, and those answers also occasionally provided me with some personal, if frightening, entertainment. For example, one of my favorite answers to the question about why the French language had been chosen was, "I LOVE French bread!" The scariest answers to the other two questions were ones like, "France is in South America" and "The capital of France is London." Responses like those let me know right away that the uphill climb that semester was going to be very steep indeed.

In addition to the beginning French class, I also had three classes of Freshman English I, with the promise from those "above" that I would be given more advanced classes in both languages after I had achieved tenure. This was always a confusing idea to me, as I thought that maybe beginning students needed seasoned instructors for inspiration and guidance as much as the advanced kids did. In any event, I was still the lowest face on the totem pole with a long way to go in showing what I could do. But, I was content.

Living only a block from the school, I did my grocery shopping at the A&P nearby, and my banking also within walking distance from my apartment. My location entailed two issues. The first was that the whole school knew where I lived, which meant that occasionally students would drop by to visit or to ask for help with current lessons that were too challenging for them to handle alone. I didn't really mind, as long as there were no visitors after seven in the evening. Nowadays such visits would probably appear scandalous, but I'm happy to say that there was never a problem, and students were polite about the visits, without exception. I think visiting teachers made students feel more grown up. It also gave them a chance for free tutoring and occasionally time for make-up tests.

The other result of my living so close to school was that in my trips to the grocery store, I almost always encountered students and their parents. This too was not such a bad thing after a while, but kids at first looked at me as though I were a fish out of water, flopping around the pier. That look on their faces said, "Oh, God! He actually buys groceries and eats food!" This was because they were so used to seeing their teachers in clouds of chalk dust, surrounded by books and papers, maybe with a map or a globe nearby, that the shock of seeing a teacher with a shopping cart in the frozen foods section of the A&P, or purchasing a box of Count Chocula cereal was almost more that they could handle.

Johnny Madison was once again in my English I class after failing it the year before, but this time he would do far better, receiving a "B" for the semester, doing well also in his art class, which displayed several of Johnny's framed oils and water colors in the school library.

A few of my students from the year before stopped by my classroom occasionally to let me know how they were doing in English. They included Deirdre, and Debbie, who was still writing poems that could clog a kitchen sink, but who wanted me to read them, " very carefully" and then critique them on paper. I am proud to say that my level of diplomacy (also known as horse hockey) in those critiques reached heights of skill that could easily have made me ambassador to any other country in the world. Debbie would bring me page after page of poetic swill that required written commentary on my part, which was usually the suggestion that she attempt more original and striking imagery. One example of her poetry had more than twenty stanzas, of which I will share only one, for those readers, who might be diabetic:

Love for Bobby
Bobby is far away,
so I feel sad today.
I miss his blue eyes
and wavy brown hair
and want him to know
how much I really care.

After reading all twenty verses of that poem and others Debbie wrote, I felt as though I had just drunk an entire bottle of Karo Syrup. My pleas for Debbie not to be quite so literal fell upon deaf ears, so that my only consolation was that her days of plagiarism had ended, even though I must confess feeling nostalgic for the truly great stuff she had been stealing only a year before.

My three freshman English classes were reading Homer's ODYSSEY, for which I felt obligated to create different quizzes and tests for each, so that students wouldn't feel the temptation to cash in on the work already having been done by other classes. All three classes did, however, share the same spelling lists, vocabulary lists, and essay topics. One kid named Roy depended solely upon his own considerable creativity to come up with vocabulary definitions on tests, rather than to learn the actual ones. An example of his originality was his definition for the word, "bullion," which he wrote was " a noun meaning much, much more than a billion." There were many pupils who had obviously coasted along in middle school to get by, and it took consistency and huge amounts of effort to convey to them the serious message that they would not be able to sneak through high school that way. Of course, my warnings and those of other teachers often did little more than inspire students to create newer and better ways to avoid work they were assigned. I have always suspected that many kids spend more time and effort getting out of school work than would be required in just doing the assignments in the first place and getting credit for them.

I remember having taken some history courses in high school and college that were duller than slate, due to the material having been reduced to battles, dates, and treaties to be memorized, never with even a reference to the music, art, cuisine, fashion, or entertainment of the eras being studied. My best history teachers had us singing songs, reading poems of the period, watching silent films from the time of World War I, discussing culture clashes of the time. Learning came to life from the creative efforts of those wonderful teachers and meant something in sensory ways in those memorable classes, and I was determined to provide such immersion, the kind I had also received in my French and Spanish classes in high school.

One of those elements was cuisine. Even in the first year class, I gave recipes for simple French bread, Madeleins (type of French cookie), and cheese souffle. That meant teaching the metric conversions and offering extra credit to those brave souls, who attempted the recipes at home. On Mardi Gras in February we would have a "fete" with dishes made by students from French recipes (in French). Spanish and German classes did this also, and we would all have a food exchange so that the Foreign Language Department smelled like a gourmet restaurant, creating happy memories for students and teachers, despite Karen Filmore's fallen French sponge cake, that everyone thought was a giant cookie.

Chapter 15 Rivalries, Cars, and Hungarians

Though I can't speak for other academic departments at MHS, I can, without hesitation, say that the faculty members of the English and Foreign Language Departments were like two families having their respective matriarchs, Winifred Mason, and Charlotte Graham, two grandes dames, one of whom had already retired, and the other on the verge. Though Miss Mason had moved on to the reward of full retirement, and Glenn had become department chair, Winifred's advice on everything from textbooks to curriculum and department policy was still sought by several in the English Department. Her wisdom and experience had been the bulwark of the best-run high school academic department in the county. She knew people and was able to size them up for their motives, sincerity and abilities as quickly as Jane Marple, and possessed the same razor-sharp intelligence, cloaked by silk blouses, tailored tweed suits, and that marvelously dignified blue-rinsed hair. She had held together the English Department through a combination of diplomacy in assigning classes, and by understanding the dynamic of rivalry among her teachers. She had given dinner parties for her department members at her own home, where criticisms and hopes among teachers were discussed openly, after which sound solutions always came about. This icon had been my mentor.

Earlier reference to department members being like a family was based upon loyalty, but also upon power struggles (i.e. "I want and deserve the English Literature class.") and sibling rivalries, some of which should have resulted in coal being left in Christmas stockings. Overall, however, mutual respect and good will were the order of the day.

The Foreign Language Department was unique in that the French, German, and Spanish, and Latin teachers were not really competing for each other's classes, except in terms of enrollment, the largest share always going to Spanish, due partly to the persistent myth that it was the easiest to learn among the four languages. It's not as though I had to stand in the halls holding posters that said, "French is better than German, Spanish, or Latin!" or "Free petits fours if you sign up for French class!" As it was for most other classes, foreign language enrollment was based most upon word of mouth among the students, who always ended up being the best marketers of classes anyway. Mrs. Graham remained aloof in most cases in order to allow her department members to work things out on their own. I don't remember ever even having a department meeting.

If there was competition between foreign language teachers, it was of a different sort. For example, Senora Mendoza, who was right across the hall from my classroom, sometimes taught her classes Spanish and Mexican folk songs. We would both usually leave our classroom doors open and compete to see whose class could sing louder. The kids loved it and always rose to the occasion, even though one day, while Senora Mendoza's class was belting out, "La Cucaracha," and my group was singing "Alouette" at top volume, our principal, Mr. Perkins, appeared in my doorway with a most perplexed expression on his face, though he said nothing.

On "El Cinco de mayo" (May 5th), Mexico celebrates its independence from the French, going back to 1862, obviously not a holiday my French classes would be celebrating. The Spanish classes, however, enjoyed fiestas with tamales, tacos, flautas and flan all day long until during my sixth period French class, I sent to Senora Mendoza, via a student messenger, a gift-wrapped package containing a French flag. We timed this delivery for my quick visit to the main office with a recording of "La Marseillaise" (French National anthem), which I played over the P.A. system only into Senora Mendoza's classroom, interrupting their singing of a "cancion ranchera." This kind of thing went on all the time, especially near the end of the school day on Fridays. Enormous fun came from these friendly and amusing attempts to outdo each other. There was sometimes thunderous laughter from each side trying to surpass the other.

Almost everyone has heard the children's Canadian French song, "Alouette," that lilting, sweet melody we sometimes hear in French films of charmingly uniformed children hiking in some lovely meadow of the Alps. The fact is, the words are rather ghastly, and involve a gentle little lark song bird and threats to pluck its feathers, and every other part from beak to liver from the poor thing. I'm surprised that PETA hasn't created an international incident about the lyric, but the deceptively melodic tune belies the violent words, and in France and Canada, singing the song is a way for small children to learn the French vocabulary for most body parts, both external and internal, depending upon how many verses are sung. For my beginning French classes, it was always a favorite for which volume increased inevitably.

Then there was the afternoon I went downstairs during my prep hour to relax a bit over coffee in the teachers' lounge, where there was only one other faculty member, sitting at a conference table reading THE WALL STREET JOURNAL. It was Jack Farrel of the Social Studies Department. Not wanting to appear aloof or snobbish in any way, I sat down with my mug of coffee at the same table, but his reaction sitting across from me was at first only to peer over the top of his newspaper and over his eyeglasses, which were halfway down his long nose. It was the scrutinizing gaze of someone, who clearly felt superior and who saw me as a creature so far down the evolutionary scale, that I was worth little more regard than a garden slug. After what seemed an interminable silence, he folded the paper, commenting, "So you're one of the probationers."

"If you mean a neophyte or novice," I answered, "then, yes, that would be me. I suppose you've been here since the Mesozoic Period?"

Through a half-smile, he answered, "Since even before that. Aren't you teaching English?"

"Yes," I responded. "And one class of French."

"Ah, two foreign languages, eh?"

"Indeed." I said.

"Well, you still have the look of an optimist, but your students will soon file that down to nothing. You newbies are all alike, coming in here with angels' wings and truck loads of hope, but then leaving after a couple of years with devils' horns, driving the then empty, old, rusty truck you started with to some other line of work."

"Don't be too sure," I said, then adding, "Any special reason you're still here?"

Grinning like the Cheshire cat, he simply replied, "Pension."

Then grabbing my coffee mug and his folded WALL STREET JOURNAL, I left the room to go back upstairs.

On the faculty of the English Department was a very different member of the staff, a tiny, delicate, almost bird-like woman named Mrs. Millicent Fowler, who had been teaching since the 1930's and whose classes I had observed during my first year on the faculty. Having also seen classes being taught by the burly, loud, brash football coach, Mr. Bennett, I was able to note the extreme contrasts between both teachers and how they conducted their classes. Cass Bennett used loudness and insults in what he considered maintaining "order." Remaining at his desk, however, he missed so much that was going on all over the room. His attempts to inspire fear had succeeded only in compelling his students to find ways to ignore or circumvent his boorish manner. Whispering was common, because Mr. Bennett was too loud to notice, and secretly exchanged notes flew about the classroom, because he wasn't observant enough to notice even half of these shenanigans. My being there as an observer didn't seem to pose any threat to the students, even though I was taking careful notes.

On the other hand, Mrs. Fowler, despite, or perhaps because of, her gentle demeanor and quiet dignity, students listened intently, hanging on every word she uttered, knowing that consequences of a different kind awaited anyone who was not paying attention. She was keenly observant with the eyes of an eagle as she walked around the room asking unexpected questions of the unwary, who might not have been tuned in to the subject matter at hand. There was something engaging about that small but enchanting voice, which even the tiniest whisper could have interrupted. Then there was the fascinating content of her talks about English literature through her intelligence, insight, and passion for it. She conveyed the powerful and reasonable message that what she was saying mattered, even if said in a quiet way. Mrs. Fowler also possessed a sharp sense of humor that made people hang onto her words, words that made the class want to be ready for some devilishly clever punchline that might otherwise be missed.

The differences between those two styles of teaching and classroom management stayed with me all the remaining years I taught, the idea that it wasn't as much about "control" as it was about encouraging the class to join me, because that would be more interesting and enjoyable than anything else the students could come up with. Blustery manner and intimidation through browbeating may have their place in a military setting or on a football field, but not in my classroom. That wasn't who I was, and it was a most valuable lesson for me to learn.

The freshman English classes continued to be a battleground, where I fought split infinitives, dangling or misplaced modifiers, double negatives, punctuation disasters, run-on sentences, fragments, and misspellings. One of my chief weapons in this struggle was the same big, wooden salad bowl I used in my French class. I would type between one and two hundred sentences, each one containing a usage or spelling error. Then I would cut the sentences with scissors into individual strips, fold them, and toss them into the bowl. The class would be divided into two teams, and I would keep score at the blackboard. There were a few pieces of paper in the bowl marked as double points, as on the TV show, Jeopardy. The result of team scores determined which side would receive ten bonus points on the next test. Such competitions were diversions and practice sessions at once. After drawing a paper from the bowl and reading the item aloud, the student had the option of challenging anyone on the opposite team he thought wasn't paying attention. The one challenged had to repeat the sentence that had just been read aloud, and if he failed to do this, an extra point was given to the challenger's team. That system worked well, because the students disciplined each other far better than I ever could in that context.

Grades in all my classes I calculated in terms of point values in order to make things more concrete. A quiz might be worth twenty points, homework fifteen, an essay fifty, and a test one hundred. These numbers were recorded daily and were always available to students to add up in order to find out their current grades. Ninety-five percent of the total possible number of points was an "A." Eighty-five percent was a "B" and so forth. Sixty-five percent was the lowest passing grade. I called my record of those points a "bank account" for each student, and at the end of each term, every student could purchase a grade according to the number of points he had earned along the way. Also there was never a moment when a student didn't know exactly, to the very point, how he was doing in the class. Likening grades to money seemed to strike a chord, making those points a kind of currency, thus connecting their value to earnings that would come later in the work place outside of school.

It was at this time that I took the bus downtown to Schmuzer Buick to look at cars, and after some feigned interest in newer models, which were entirely out of my price range, I purchased a 1966 Buick Le Sabre in a soft, eggnog yellow with a luxurious black interior and an engine as quiet as a pocket watch. Upwardly mobile as I may have felt, it should be remembered that my net income each month was only $452 and my car payment was $53, which didn't include gasoline, insurance and maintenance costs, but none of that really mattered to me. I had a car, and even though I continued walking to and from school most days, I enjoyed waving at the bus, which I would never have to ride again. Seeing that beautiful car for the first time took my mind back to the morning of my twelfth birthday, when I had received a J. C. Higgins bicycle. Like that bike, the car made me feel terrifically empowered by the sense of mobility, which made it so much easier to do grocery shopping and trips to the library. For a man (and perhaps for a woman too), owning that first car is a pinnacle of independence, and I gloried in it.

One morning, Mrs. Fitzsimmons, a school counselor, brought to my classroom a new student from Hungary, who had been in the United States for only two days and still had the look of a rabbit facing a ravenous coyote. His name was Octavian, he was sixteen years old, and was being placed in my freshman English class, presumably on the grounds that I taught a foreign language. To our school counselors, the same logic would have applied to anyone who was Chinese, Greek, or Russian. I imagine now the possible confab those counselors might have had about any such new foreign student.

"Yes, he's Hungarian, but Bolinger teaches French, which is a foreign language too. Yeah, just send the kid up to Bolinger's room." The same logic might have been represented had one of the counselors suggested that Octavian be taken directly to the school cafeteria, because it was serving goulash that afternoon. However, we teachers rarely contested decisions made by the counselors, who were another breed of human kind, that lived in the lower regions of that first floor behind the main office, rarely seeing the light of day. We sometimes called them "the mushroom people." We feared them only because they had the power to recommend our classes to increase our enrollment. In any event, there stood Mrs. Fitzsimmons, who simply introduced Octavian by his first name and left the poor boy, who knew not a word of English, standing in the hallway outside my classroom, where he may not even have been aware he was to be studying English. A handsome, dark-haired boy, he was wearing a leopard skin vest over a brightly colored yellow shirt, black leather pants, and European boots with fur tops, all of which were about to make a very striking impression, good or bad, upon my second period freshmen.

Chapter 16 New Doors Opening

The opening door has always been a symbol of welcome and of opportunity, though I doubt that Octavian saw it either way that morning I opened the door to room 248 and led him through rows of turning heads, gazing eyes, and several half-stifled giggles of the English I second period class. Having just arrived from a completely different culture, Octavian certainly had an appearance that those freshmen saw as somewhat incompatible with their own. His hair was considerably longer than that of the other boys, and his clothing made a much bolder and more exotic statement than any of the conservative, button-down collars and other reactionary fashions current in the Northwest Indiana of 1970. Five years later Octavian's style would be the norm, but at the time of his arrival to America, he was a blazing neon bulb among the quiet night lights of Hammond. There was never an explanation of Octavian's move to the United States, except over some kind of political strife that had forced him and his parents to escape Hungary and to live with his uncle in the States. It was said that his uncle knew some English, so I was relieved that Octavian might hear at least some of our language at home.

I introduced him as a student newly arrived from Hungary and said that he would need all of our help in learning English. Because I didn't want him to stand there too long, as though on display at a carnival, I added only that I hoped all in the class could begin to imagine how difficult it might be to be suddenly placed in a country and not knowing its language. All eyes followed as I led him to the only empty seat left, which was in the back of the room. He continued to smile and nod, almost as though he understood perfectly what was going on, and in a heavy accent, he said, "Thank you."

Hearing some snickering continue on the other side of the room, I knew I had to use the opportunity to comment on such insensitivity without making it a kind of punishment that might bring about retaliation directed against the innocent Octavian. I reminded the class that the world was far bigger than they imagined, and that there were many other kinds of music, food, fashions, and languages, no particular one claiming any sort of superiority among the rest. I said that though America had been influenced by European countries and their ways, those other countries were much older than we were and that no one of them needed be considered out of step, because differences could be not only allowed, but respected. That's what America was all about.

Continuing on the theme of tolerance, I told the class that despite what may have been their rigid belief that we were the best, Hammond was far from being the hub of the universe or the standard of anything, especially fashion. Not wanting all this to become a long snooze of a lecture, I ended by saying that rather than remaining full of ourselves at how great we thought we were, we actually all had a lot to learn from this new student and he from us. From the back of the room Octavian only smiled, but the snickering stopped.

Before the end of class, I asked two other students whom I trusted for their sensitivity and intelligence to take Octavian under their wing to show him the ropes, have lunch with him, and generally to be his mentors in whatever ways they could. They seemed happy to do this and walked with him to his next class. As they all three grew smaller in their long walk together down the corridor, I continued to hear Octavian's broken "Thank you."

Teenagers, as they stumble through the vast maze of learning the social graces, can be, in turn, both infuriating and hyper-sensitive. They don't always learn good behavior at home, so we have to remember that they remain sometimes for long periods in a state of trying to imitate what they think is currently, "cool" and that a confident and comfortable individuality, coupled with a true social conscience can take many years. What we like to call "grown up" behavior can often go on hiatus during parts of adolescence.

A teenager's world is often a fragile place with erratic extremes of inappropriate boldness from a fearless belief that there are no consequences worth noting, to feelings of terror at doing the wrong thing, taking the wrong step. Our egos as teens are as delicate as they will ever be, assaulted on all fronts to grow up, be responsible, do homework, keep up grades, respect elders, choose better role models, wear the right clothes, fit in with peers, be more independent, and to address romantic yearnings without going too far. Boys are taught to take chances and then criticized if they fail. Girls are encouraged to play it safe by not taking risks. As teens we always like to believe that we know more about ourselves and the world than we actually know. Our confidence can shrink and immobilize us at parties or in classes where we are terrified of blundering and being overwhelmed by our greatest fear of all, not fitting in with our classmates. Or, we can delete common sense at times to soar in a dizzying but very temporary, wild abandon before being hurt or humiliated in our early encounters with cars, alcohol, or the opposite sex.

As teens we often feel the world's critical and suspicious eye and the likelihood that we will not be respected or even tolerated for what we think. Not being taken seriously is the worst curse of being a teen. Adults often see us merely as hormones with shoes. Maybe that's why finding a personal talent for doing something well means so much to us at that time of life. Sports, music (even our personal choices of music), clothes, are all elements of a teenager's quest for personal identity, that terrible need to fit in while holding tightly to whatever turns out to be what makes us unique individuals, even if it turns out to be tattoos, spiked blue hair, nose rings, or other piercings or body modifications that at age forty will look absurd and regrettable. It is that ephemeral little world that teens inhabit, rejoice and suffer in, and spend all their adolescent energies trying to escape.

Because Octavian had not brought with him any school records in English, there was no way yet for me to know anything about his academic abilities until discovering by accident that he had already studied French for two years. As I walked by his desk, I noticed some French sentences he had been writing in his notebook. This opened up a new way to help him with his English and to have him enrolled in Mrs. Graham's third-year French class right away.

I made a large felt-covered board and began cutting out hundreds of pictures from magazines and gluing them to pieces of cardboard to stabilize them before adhering fragments of more felt. This served as a story board to which we could add pictures to create narratives about daily life for learning vocabulary and verb usage. Everyday after school I would work with Octavian in creating stories and having him keep a notebook for English verb conjugations and other vocabulary. We had also a Hungarian/English dictionary and a French/English one.

Of course, he was already picking up many English words in other classes, in the halls, on television, and in the cafeteria, some words I had hoped he wouldn't be learning. Another student at lunch one day thought it might be funny to teach him some foul words and then encourage Octavian to sound "more American" by using them in his classes to impress his peers. After shocking his teachers, one by one, with interjections of words that would make a Longshoreman hide his face, the stream of highly inappropriate vocabulary was traced back to a kid in Octavian's lunch hour, who was given three morning detentions for his tutoring efforts. In spite of the apparently long list of "bad" words added to Octavian's working vocabulary, we were all gratified to know what a quick learner he was and what a phenomenal memory he possessed.

Between classes I usually stood in the hallway outside my room to help make sure things were orderly. Other teachers did the same so that faculty visibility made a difference in preventing fights and getting kids to their classes on time. However, just around the corner in Locker Bay D, I discovered an area where a few boys and their girl friends were having make-out sessions that sounded like a plumbers' convention demonstrating the efficiency of kitchen plungers. Passing time between classes being only five minutes meant that these amorous diversions had to be done very fast in order for the students to be on time to their next classes. My breaking up these kissing interludes brought me some fake apologies and a few red faces, but for three or four couples, those words of repentance faded overnight, so that the next day I would find them again at "Lovers' Point" in the same locker bay, practicing their osculation skills.

When even the threat of detentions had little if any effect, and lip smacking sounds continued to resound from that area, I brought to school my Minolta SRT 200 35mm camera. There wasn't even any film in the camera, but my purpose was to startle the couples so badly, that they would never consider returning to that area, let alone indulge in the passionate smooching that had become such a habit. When I entered the locker bay the next time to find the same remaining couples glued to each other's lips, I aimed my camera, pretending to focus, saying, "Hey! Can you move a little to your left for this shot? Oh wait, that's a good one. Perfect! Do you think your parents would like some eight-by-ten glossies of these?"

The looks on their faces went beyond what can be summoned by words like shock or terror. The students seemed absolutely paralyzed by fear. In a couple of days the problem was completely gone, at least from Locker bay D. It's entirely possible that those orgiastic displays had simply been relocated to some other locker bay area, but I suspect the true catalyst was the frightening message passed quickly along of, "Don't make-out in Locker Bay D. That weird mustard and ketchup teacher'll take your pictures and send 'em to your parents!" I have to admit that I felt proud of finding a solution to another problem never covered by any of my college methods classes.

Meanwhile, Octavian's English was improving daily, and other students seemed to be accepting him socially as one of their own, and many of the girls found him to be very attractive, partly from his good looks, but also because of his charming, Hungarian accent that must have seemed quite exotic to the teenage girls of Northwest Indiana. He was also learning about American fashion, at least to the extent that he was beginning to dress like the other boys and cut his hair in a more regional way. It was a bit sad that he seemed to have sacrificed some of his individuality by conforming for the sake of acceptance, but he appeared to be happy not to appear as foreign as he had upon his arrival in this country, and I guess it should be remembered how important it is during those teen years to fit in, something that maybe most of us never get over, no matter how old we are. In any case, Octavian was enjoying America.

Chapter 17 Diversion

Not every moment of school for students or teachers will be exactly titillating. There will be times when drill and practice in areas like punctuation or spelling can be anesthetizing for some kids. There can't be dancing bears every minute of every day in the classroom, and the teacher can't wear his top hat and tap shoes all the time. Occasionally it's going to be hard work and sweat in learning those skills necessary to function in a work environment that won't always be Disney World either. Kids need to find their own solutions through critical thinking about the world in which they live, and the whole world is the body of a teacher's resources. Anything and everything that relates to lesson material is fair game for reinforcement. A new teacher should expect to spend at least an hour a day planning lessons, depending on the number of preps he has. With between one hundred-twenty and one hundred-fifty students per day, there may also be lots of other paper work in teaching academic subjects. English is probably the most time consuming because of those stacks of themes and essays. With all due respect to teachers of physical education and industrial arts, a three-page composition will take more time to grade than a push-up or a bread board. I didn't mean for that to sound bitter. Teachers must also allow themselves time for sleeping, bathing, and eating from time to time.

One thing that helps to keep the wheels turning at school is humor. Used in the right ways and at the right times, it can lighten the spirit, make people feel more at ease, and often even disarm tricky situations that could otherwise be far more troublesome. Humor can help students look forward to classes, but it helps teachers too. I remember wearing a camel hair sports coat one day to school, and a student named Jeff came to the front of the French class right after the bell rang to place on my lapel a large, round paper logo he had made with crayon that said, "CENTURY 21." It was perfect, and I laughed so hard, that I had to sit down to catch my breath. The class loved it too. There was a mutual respect and affection that allowed that flight of fancy, and when a class is blessed with a sense of fun, that gift should be embraced and cherished.

In another French class was a fellow named Steve, who was a bundle of energy, who had trouble sitting still. This was before the label of Attention Deficit Disorder, so I don't really know if his antsy behavior was an ailment. Nowadays there are too many such labels being thrown around like confetti. Steve was bright, cooperative, and quite funny, even though Nancy, a girl he liked very much, sat on the other side of the room, where Steve's attention was sometimes diverted by his utter enchantment with that girl. One day I gave the class a ten-minute written activity on irregular French verbs to complete and said that I needed to go to the main office for just a few minutes. I added that no one should leave his seat for any reason, upon pain of death at my return. I saw Steve's eyes move toward Nancy's desk in the forbidden zip code of the other side of the class. In the main office I used the P.A. system, saying into the microphone (only to my classroom), "Stephen, you get back to your seat right now!" The office staff was always willing to be in on these things with me and howled with laughter when we heard Steve knocking over chairs in his rush to get back to his own desk from the other side of the room, where I knew he had been visiting Nancy. When I returned to room 248, the entire class, except Nancy, was guffawing. She had her head down at her desk, trying to disappear.

Some of the faculty were unsurprisingly straight-laced and probably hadn't even chuckled since the end of world War II, but others were usually up for anything on the outrageous side. For example, There was a faculty party at the beach home of the parents of one of the shop teachers, where there was lots of good food, along with wines of varying levels of quality. As the evening unfolded, Jack Farrel of the Social Studies Department became more and more pretentious about his knowledge of wines, spouting terms about "woodsy tones," "heady bouquets," and "fruity essences." He stood behind the bar as if he were at a lectern giving valuable and badly needed information to us poor, ignorant peasants.

His taking a break from his pontificating to go to the rest room left an opening for Cliff, one of the shop teachers, who had brought as a joke a bottle of the cheapest and vilest wine, which I believe was called Swizzle, far less expensive even than soda pop. Cliff poured one of the "expensive" French wines into a pitcher and filled the then empty bottle with the Swizzle. When Jack stumbled back into the room to continue his discourse on fine wines, Cliff asked him to expound upon the differences between American and French vintages. Always ready to show off by belittling individuals or entire countries, Jack began to rhapsodize upon the bottle of what he believed was a French burgundy, complimenting its "rich, ruby color" and "savory overtones," while sniffing and tasting something that could easily have been used to clean windows. Needless to say, the room was filled with stifled giggles that became almost hysterical laughter after Jack finally passed out on a leather sofa from which he later peeled himself to go home.

For some unknown reason, such conspiratorial practical jokes appealed to me wildly and still do, sometimes because while being funny, they also dispense a kind of justice in quarters where it is most merited, There was no one on the faculty, who had not suffered the cruel barbs issued by Jack Farrel. Thus, the supreme gratification we all felt when his insincerity and snobbishness were exposed in such an efficient way, his having done practically the whole job for us. It was poetic.

There came a point, where the morning announcements read to us over the P.A. system were becoming duller than old dish water, and students, along with their homeroom teachers were simply tuning out, as though one could actually see in their eyes an illuminated dial that was switching stations as soon as the P.A. clicked on with Mr. Poteja's "Thought for today." With the help of some good-humored co-conspirators in the main office, I began adding one fake announcement per day, an announcement that was totally ridiculous after Mr. Poteja's "thought" (He had only one, I believe).

An example of this nonsense was, "Attention students: tryouts for our stage production of THE POSEIDON ADVENTURE will be after school next Wednesday. Please bring snorkels or pressurized diving suits." Another example was, "Attention students: the detention room will no longer be used. From now on, instead of staying after school, student offenders will be deported to the Siberian Tundra or the Norther Irish Peat Bogs, with no lunch money."

Another was, "Attention faculty and students: There will be a session after school Thursday for volunteers to make for our cheerleaders a new set of pom-poms from the many strands of hair Mr. Powers has been losing lately. Come one, come all." In about a week, people began paying more attention to the morning announcements, waiting for the one absurd one that could be read at any time between the real ones.

In THE HAMMOND TIMES there appeared a brief story about the current president of the Whiting Polish Catholic Women's League (Jenska Yednota). Her name was Sophie Greshko. Whiting was the home of one of my childhood acquaintances, Eddie Pooplava, whom some of his "friends" tied to the railroad tracks near Standard Oil when we were kids. His escape was the stuff of legend, so that everything about Whiting, Indiana held a fascination for me ever after. In any case, I knew that I had to use Sophie's name for something.

In those days attendance was taken by placing a "pink slip" with names of absentees outside one's classroom door. Computers were yet far down the road, so one day I wrote the name Sophie Greshko on the pink slip just to see what might happen. When her name appeared on the master absentee list for that day, I knew I was on to something and that Sophie might , like Eddie Pooplava, achieve legendary status. As time passed (years, actually) I would occasionally submit her name as recipient of an award for Foreign Language Club, Quill and Scroll, and Girls' track. At a student awards dinner at Teibel's Restaurant in Schererville, Indiana, Sophie received a little trophy as most valuable member of the Chess Club, which I was currently sponsoring. Mr. Perkins, our principal, presented the awards, and of course, I had to accept Sophie's for her, as she was unable to attend that night. Her name continued to appear occasionally in the school newspaper for honor roll, and in the year book for Knitting Club. Only certain faculty members knew about the charade, which managed to last for several years

The most outrageous part of the longterm deception about Sophie happened at the end of first semester one year after final exams, when students were not at school for two days, while faculty calculated semester grades and credits. That time the co-conspirator was none other than my maternal grandmother. Grandma Starks lived not far from the school and was a brilliant mimic, whose sense of humor and fun was positively unrivaled. She loved practical jokes and was incomparably quick in getting and playing them. Grandma agreed to phone the school (before caller ID), pretending to be Sophie's mother. The main office receptionist that day must have been startled to receive the phone call from my grandmother, who in a beautifully feigned Polish accent filled with urgency and interjection and rolled "r's", said, "Allo, dis is Morton High School, yeah? Dis is Meesus Greshko, and I vant my daughter come home rrright away, you hear? She good for notting and no makka da beds today but she at school helping da teachers. If you don't tell her come home now, I come to school and makka da big stink in office, yeah?" That's apparently all it took. The next thing I knew, the P.A. system for the whole school was blaring the announcement, "Will Sophie Greshko please report to the main office immediately. Your mother wants you to go home right away." The message was given three times in ten minutes, and there were howls of laughter coming from classrooms of teachers, who knew the facts about Sophie Greshko.

The jig finally came to a sad end, when at the end of another semester years later, I sent a note, via student messenger, to the main office with the message that Sophie should be paged at once and report to the gym. I emphasized to the messenger that under no circumstance should he reveal the source of the page and that he should just say that it had come from "some teacher on the first floor." Such subterfuge! I blush now to think how low I had sunk to keep the Sophie legend afloat. It seems that the no-nonsense Mrs. Alexander was behind the counter that afternoon when the note was delivered. I was told later that she screamed, "Who gave you this note?" Evidently, the kid buckled instantly to blurt out, "Mr. Bolinger." Mrs. Alexander called me down to the main office, where she was standing behind the long counter, her arms folded, and a look of extreme displeasure on her face. Her statement to me was only half funny. "I've been seeing and hearing this girl's name around here for at least eight years. Is there more than one? I was beginning to think she must be on the faculty. What's going on?" Thus came about Sophie's demise...or graduation. She was never heard from again, except in recollections of the old guard of faculty, who still remembered her and smiled at the sound of her name. Jack Farrel's comment to me was simply, "You really need to get out more, John."

I end this chapter with reference to a colossal practical joke of which I was the butt. Shopping at the A&P one warm spring evening, I was shocked to see on the entrance bulletin board of local announcements an enormous poster with the message, in huge black felt marker letters, "PLEASE HELP SEND THIS CHILD TO SUMMER CAMP! A poor orphan from the age of three, Buddy also lost his foster parents from pneumonia. Give if you can."

Then I saw a childhood photo of me, wearing a crooked bow tie and a silly grin, Underneath the photo in big, fat digits, was my phone number and the final message, "CALL THIS NUMBER TO MAKE YOUR DONATION. THANK YOU."
Two of my friends from the English Department had done the whole thing, and I felt mortified as I stood there between the store's two sets of electric doors, wearing shorts and my stupid corduroy slippers, shoppers around me mumbling for me to get out of their ways as they rolled their carts past me.

There were actually some fake phone calls later that night from other faculty members pretending large offers of money to send me to camp. The intervening years have made it much more hilarious to me than it was that night.

I guess the point I've been trying to make is that life sails by so very fast but can be perked up by laughter. It has its place in school too and can bring joy to everyone, except maybe principals like Mr. Perkins, or office matrons, like Mrs. Alexander.

Chapter 18 Way of the World

After Charlotte Graham retired, I inherited her French classes, so that I would be teaching two English classes, and three of French. Charlotte had enjoyed a prep period, plus another period for department business, which pretty much meant flirting with male faculty members in the lounge and drinking French blend over shared gossip and coffee cake. The German teacher, Herr Schutz, because of his seniority, became chair. I was to teach two freshman English classes, a first-year French class, a second-year French class, and a combined third and fourth-year French class, the schedule amounting really to five preparations, though the school logic was that combining two levels using different text books, lesson plans, and tests was just all French anyway so as to be considered by the administration as only one prep. In fact, any teacher, who had only one prep all day was paid the same amount as a teacher who had five preps. This was like a man loading five tons of bricks in a day being paid the same amount as another man loading only one ton of the same bricks.

Though things are now changing for the better regarding teacher pay, taking into consideration his duties and successes, in those days I sometimes thought the system of teacher pay a strange one and cannot even now think of any other profession that espouses such a sloppy way of clumping duties together, based solely upon hours one is in a building. Of course, the only other profession with such high expectations of selfless dedication and charitable duty is the clergy. Lawyers, doctors, engineers, architects, and accountants would never dream of suffering the abuses of heavy work loads every evening, including weekends, without proper monetary compensation. I know that the best teachers have always been those who gave generously of their time and talents for the sake of imparting knowledge to kids, who needed and wanted that knowledge, but I've never understood why these talented people couldn't also be paid something more as a kind of bonus, added to the glow of comprehension or inspiration on a student's face.

Teacher evaluations were done by our school administrators, Mr. Perkins, principal, and Mr. Poteja, assistant principal. I don't want to be unfair about their methods, because I never had to give formal judgments about anyone but my students. The written and oral evaluations I was given all the years I taught were always glowing ones, but I might have taken them more seriously, had they been more detailed and based upon very careful and sincere observation.

One teacher evaluation I recall vividly occurred one afternoon in my advanced French class, the one that was split into two groups. The fourth year and I were discussing in French a short story by Balzac that they had read, and the third-year class was writing a brief commentary in French on LE PETIT PRINCE, a book by St. Exupery. No English was spoken. During the discussion, Mr. Poteja entered the classroom, sat down with a notebook in which he wrote very little before opening the sports section of THE TIMES, in which he became engrossed for the next fifteen minutes, until all my students quickly and quietly left the room, heading for the foreign language lab, where both groups were to have their weekly sessions of listening and speaking drill from their individual booths. Still completely occupied by his newspaper, Mr. Poteja needed a tap on the shoulder to let him know that the students were gone, and that he was welcome to join them in the lab. His cartoon facial expression of, "Which way did they go?" and curt response of, "No, that won't be necessary," told me all I needed to know about his level of interest. Though I remain sympathetic with him for his having to evaluate a class conducted in a language he didn't understand, I suppose I expected him to pick up on the rapport between me and my students, and to notice their responsiveness, splendid behavior, and the interaction between us. It still strikes me as absolutely rude that he spent most of his visit disconnected from us by reading a newspaper, but over time I became accustomed to the insensitive behavior of clods, like him, who were usually the ones who became administrators in the first place.

The other evaluation that will remain forever in my memory was conducted by Mr. Perkins, the principal, for my first-year French class. Mr. Powell, the carpenter father of one of my students, Laurie Powell, kindly built me a puppet theater of plywood painted with a pale green enamel. The three sides were hinged, so that after removing the top, the whole thing could be easily folded for storage. On either side of the two-by three foot opening in front was a cut-out plywood mask painted white, one for comedy, and the other for tragedy. Inside was a curtain rod with cranberry-colored curtains made by Laurie's mother, and another rod at the back of the stage area for hanging painted scenery. It was a splendid device for classroom use. Students created sock puppets, and some brought in professionally made ones. Wigs, mustaches, hats, clothing, and rolled up paper backdrops eventually filled one of the cabinets in my classroom.

One day, while three students inside the puppet theater were doing a kind of Punch and Judy skit they had written in French, Mr. Perkins walked in with his notebook, sat in the back of the room, and put on his glasses to observe. He always had the look of those buxom, matronly women in old movies, who examined people through pince-nez spectacles as though the people they were scrutinizing were in some way inferior beings. The whole class was riveted by what the puppets were doing, and most students didn't even notice the "stranger" in our midst. The puppet show was loud and slap stick, but not slapdash, and it was in French that was very respectably pronounced. Mr. Perkins registered no facial expression at all, until one of the puppeteers moved carelessly and quickly too far to his right, dislodging the little theater's roof, which came crashing down on the three performers, only one button-eyed sock face sticking out from the rubble. No one was hurt, but I felt awful that the one day the principal paid a visit, we would have to endure such a comic disaster. The rest of the class began to laugh hysterically, one kid on the floor, doubled over, tickled beyond repair, and surprisingly, Mr. Perkins had such a big smile, that he actually covered his face with his hands, as if he were somehow embarrassed at enjoying himself. That evaluation was the best one I ever had.

There was at that time a disturbing development in the arrival of two new substitute teachers, one a semi-permanent replacement for our band director, Mrs. Brom, and the other, a regular sub who generally taught English classes. In fact, most substitute teachers were mere babysitters, who did not really instruct classes over which they were given charge, but rather became proctors, who turned everything into study halls, concerned mainly with just surviving the day. There were exceptions among the subs, of course, who followed the carefully and often lovingly written lesson plans left by teachers who wanted their classes to continue without any serious interruptions. One sub always carried a notebook with the message in big letters on the cover, "SUBS ARE NOT BOATS OR SANDWICHES. WE ARE PEOPLE TOO!"

The band substitute teacher, Mr. Sawyer, was a man with hair only along the sides of his head, especially over the ears, which appeared to be the only fertile source of his brown thatch. His stomach seemed to pour over his belt to give him a rotund midsection that reminded me of the blow-up punching bags we enjoyed as kids. Whenever I saw him, I thought of the children's commercial, "Weebles wobble, but they don't fall down." The man was obnoxious to students and faculty alike, sneering at them in a manner I suspect he thought was funny. Whenever he saw a female teacher in the halls or in the teachers' lounge, he would bark loudly, like a badly trained dog. Women would flinch but say nothing, in fear of this maniac, who treated everyone so rudely, but Mr. Sawyer was kept on, because there was evidently no other band teacher available during those weeks that Mrs. Brom was ill. However, when one morning Mr. Sawyer barked in the lounge at gentle and tiny Mrs. Fowler, the teacher of English Literature, she began putting dog biscuits and chew sticks into his mail box, and his yelping stopped for good. Students threw a welcome home party upon Mrs. Brom's return, ecstatic over the departure of the coarse and ill bred Mr. Sawyer.

The other sub, Mr. Will Chambers, was a polite, intelligent man of striking height, six feet-six inches, and though he had movie-star good looks and a commanding knowledge of material in every class he taught, he was not a success and didn't last more than a few weeks before the school system simply stopped requesting him as a temporary replacement for teachers all over the city. When I spoke with him for the first time one day at lunch, I learned why. The man had the voice of a small child. It seems his vocal chords had not kept up with the rest of his growth, and when he spoke, the timbre, depth, and tone of his speech suggested the vocal intonations of a boy in kindergarten. As articulate as he was, the first time he spoke to me, I thought he was joking by performing some kind of ventriloquist stunt. When I found out that he wasn't kidding, my heart went out to him, as I imagined what it might be like for students to see this man glide elegantly and majestically to the front of a classroom, expecting him to sound like Paul Robson or James Earl Jones, only to discover he had the voice of Minnie Mouse. I always wondered afterward what Will might have found as a career, assuming that unless he had an office job that required no speaking, he might have made a fortune doing voice-overs for cartoons.

Because I was sponsor of Foreign Language Club, I helped start a tradition in our community with what we called the International Dinner. The club had over seventy members at any given time, from all four languages, who helped advertise the dinners, which served ethnic foods from around the world. We used the cafeteria, where several tables would hold all the food for the huge buffet, admission being a covered and labeled ethnic dish or $2.50. There was also entertainment of "music from around the world" performed by students, parents, combos, and anyone else who wanted to enthrall us with music from ethnic groups, including folk songs. There was marvelous food from everywhere from Mexico to Sri Lanka, and there was always a huge attendance, filling up the cafeteria and commons area. We used cafeteria dishes and silverware, custodial staff doing some overtime. Local newspapers and the local radio station, WJOB, helped us get the word out about what we were doing.

Any money made was used to help finance field trips for foreign language classes. The great success of those dinners lasted about ten years until it just became too difficult to pull everything together, but while they lasted, they helped bring neighborhoods around the school together for an enjoyable, common purpose. At our final International Dinner, even our English Department chair, Glenn Bockman, brought English roast beef and Yorkshire pudding. Those were great times.

I received a letter near the end of first semester from my French friend, Claudine Dupont, who was finishing her work at the University of Lyon with a chance to visit America on a teaching grant and to be part a of high school life here by lecturing about her country to French classes. She chose Hammond to be her center, so I arranged for her accommodation with a family in a neighborhood of Morton High School. Claudine would be here for eight weeks to teach us about France while learning about America. She would be arriving in January, which meant I had only three weeks to practice some French recipes, which worried me a bit, since my crepes were still turning out like little bath mats.

Chapter 19 France Comes to Indiana

The new semester began with a snow storm of grand proportions, not so unusual for Northwest Indiana in January, but because I lived only a block from school, I found walking there for a couple of days easier than driving. I left my car, covered in ten inches of ice and snow, in my parking space at the apartment complex, where it seemed easier to let the sun do its work instead of my having to shovel and scrape myself into a frenzy. Those first two days of second semester, there were too many tardies to keep track of, due to the long lines of cars dropping off kids in the school parking lot. A few teachers straggled in as well. The halls were puddled by melting snow and ice, but I enjoyed the view from the southern wall of windows in my classroom, which looked out over the track and football fields, both pristine vistas of newly fallen snow with the white-capped trees in the forest beyond, a perfect backdrop for teaching my freshmen English classes Jack London's short story, "To Build a Fire" and his book, "Call of the Wild."

A new development in technology in Hammond schools was video recording equipment, purchased for use by teachers and kept in the offices and storage rooms of the school city's ware house, located just behind Morton High. Having attended a demonstration session given my the city's media chair, Mrs. Fran Gibbons, I was ready to begin using the machines to record the skits written and performed by my French classes.

The Sony equipment, which by today's standard's would seem primitive, bulky, and difficult to operate, included a large, heavy, reel to reel video tape machine, a microphone, a clumsy-looking camera on a tripod, and a television monitor, all of which resembled weaponry that might be used in some military operation to fend off enemy troops. The tapes recorded only in black and white. There was a sign-up sheet for use of these machines, and it was up to the teacher borrowing them to load them into his own car. We were usually allowed to use the equipment for two weeks at a time before having to return it for the next teacher on the sign-up sheet. Even before reserving all that stuff, I worked with students of the French classes on creating scripts of three to five minutes for groups of three to four on each production. The scripts were to include stage directions, French dialogue, and lists of props. The names of participants for each skit were written on a piece of paper, which was folded with all the others and placed into the "salad bowl." A drawing from those papers gave us our filming schedule. Background music and sound effects were chosen by each group, and credits were created on poster paper with felt markers. I worked the camera and sound. An assistant to help with off-camera work was also given to each group for their production. Students were expected to rehearse at home with their groups, but allowing for a practice run at school and several retakes, each production took an average of half an hour to complete. This activity was among those that students loved the most, and we always followed up with our own "Academy Awards."

At the Ben Franklin Five and Dime Store in Hessville, I found some little plastic statues that I spray-painted gold to simulate the Oscars. Our categories included such things as best script, best pronunciation, best staging, funniest story, best actor, and best actress. We made a voting sheet given to students in other classes for making their choices after seeing the videos, before I tallied the results. At the end of the project, we had an Academy Awards ceremony, which was always hilarious to observe, partly because students took it far more seriously than I had ever imagined they would. Those were among my happiest times in the classroom. The filming part became much easier over the years, when the equipment became much more streamlined. Also, our later skits were taped in color. Maybe the best part of those skits was that even shy students seemed unafraid to let go in being as silly as everyone else. The laughter was infectious and always of good nature.

Fortunately, the heavy snow stopped, and roads were more accessible for Claudine's arrival at O'Hare Airport in Chicago, where I picked her up that cold Saturday morning in late January. I saw her beautiful red hair bobbing among the other passengers disembarking the plane. Her hair had been cut to a kind of bob that bounced playfully as she walked and accentuated her high cheek bones and brilliant smile. Though we had continued writing each other, it was good to exchange news in person again. Claudine had not yet entered law school, because she wanted to complete her masters in international cultural affairs, in order to help open doors to international law. She seemed thrilled to have the chance to practice her English, but I was thrilled that my students would have further practice for their French. At least part of the reason she had chosen Northwest Indiana for her writing subject matter was that it was not unlike the blue-collar, middle class region in Dijon, where she had grown up and where her father had worked in a mustard processing plant. I had hoped too that I might have been at least part of her reason to choose Hammond, which was not exactly one of the world's cultural meccas.

Claudine would be spending eight weeks giving talks about France to high school classes of Northwest Indiana and observing various classes in those same schools for a paper she was writing on public education in the United States. She was even to be given tours of Hammond and surrounding towns, including Gary and its steel factories. One thing I've learned is that almost nowhere one travels need be dull, as long as it is different from one's home. Differences make travel interesting, and this was proven to me when Claudine was sincerely fascinated by Hammond and by Indiana, which I was already so used to, that it had lost much of the luster it had shown when I was younger. She seemed to get along well with everyone she met, and people loved meeting this lovely, French woman, who must have seemed rather exotic with her romantic accent, flaming red hair, and emerald green eyes. Local newspapers and the local radio station wanted to interview her, and she became something of a celebrity among all those Hammondites. She stayed at the home of Mr. and Mrs. Henry Turner, whose children attended Morton, and who lived very near the school, though I usually gave Claudine rides to and from MHS.

Everywhere Claudine went she felt welcome, which made me feel proud of Hoosier hospitality, even though we didn't have a Louvre or an Eiffel Tower. She also managed to win over almost all of the students in my French classes, except for three or four girls, who were apparently jealous of all the attention Mademoiselle Dupont was receiving from boys in those classes, Roger Mosely being the most ardent, when upon Claudine's arrival, his eyes became the size of pancakes. His growing and hopeless crush on her lasted for the entire eight weeks she was there, his body posture changing so that he leaned forward in his desk until it was usually on the verge of tipping over, all from a fear of possibly missing any whisper that might come from her lips. Roger wasn't the only one to trip over himself in undisguised adoration for this exotic creature with the alluring accent, but I couldn't fault them for their feelings, mainly because the only real difference between those boys and me was that I had learned to disguise true emotions so masterfully, that I sometimes managed to deceive even myself. I suppose that's part of our definition for being truly "grown-up," that ability to hide our true emotions, so as not to make any waves. In fact, the only waves I'd be making if I wasn't careful, would be ones signaling goodbyes at the air port, as Claudine's plane grew ever smaller in the distance.

It was mid-March when the Turner family invited me to dinner, as the end of Claudine's visit to America would be drawing to a close in only two more weeks. A sense of urgency gripped me, because my fear of rejection had prevented me from expressing that I really liked Claudine more than I had revealed before. Though we had attended movies, dinner parties, plays, concerts, and been bowling, roller skating, and had spent evenings just in conversation, I couldn't pick up on any romantic vibes from her. Laughter sometimes has a way of putting people so at ease that they see no serious overtones. My making jokes about so many things along the way had succeeded in creating a safety net for me, while also producing over several weeks what might be called a net of separation between me and what might have been more important than I realized.

Those two weeks flew by, while Claudine finished the long paper she had been writing about her experiences in America, a paper that would complete her work on the master's degree from the University of Lyon. Her plan was then to enter a law school in Paris. Our worlds were too different from each other, even just in terms of physical distance one from the other. What would I do in Paris? What would Claudine do in Northwest Indiana? All my thoughts in this matter were based upon some imagined personal connection, one that might actually have shocked or embarrassed Claudine and severed whatever friendship we had formed and enjoyed over the months since our meeting in Paris. Of course, this was all supposition on my part, based upon a similar crush I had had in high school on another girl named Barbara, a beautiful and talented pianist, who, even though we dated for two years had remained cool and aloof, above many of my imagined feelings about my own inferiority. I still often wonder how many relationships have collapsed under the weight of uncertainty or fear on the part of one person in the couple that he or she is somehow not worthy of the other.

I continued to tell, if not convince, myself that I was wearing the rose-colored glasses, that I was seeing only what I wanted to see, and that expecting more than I already had might be unrealistic, greedy, and might just destroy what was already there, safe and comfortable in a friendship that was like a cone with two scoops of wonderful ice cream, two more scoops of which might make the whole thing tumble to the ground, leaving only the empty cone.

My French classes, who had also fallen in love with Claudine, said their goodbyes on her last day at school, giving her cards with messages written in their sometimes faulty French. The advanced class had a cake that said, "Nous vous aimons beaucoup" (We like you a lot), which managed to bring tears from her, followed by laughter, when Roger Mosely gave her his gift, a pocket French/English dictionary with his photo, surrounded by tiny hearts, taped to the cover.

Driving Claudine to O'Hare Airport that cold, windy Saturday morning in late March was an emotional experience for me, though I'm not so sure it was for her. The sentimental thoughts still in my mind and heart gradually reduced themselves to the comfortable small-talk that appeared to be successful in masquerading my sadness at Claudine's departure. I felt like such an impostor, and after we kissed each other goodbye, I watched her at the boarding gate turn around once more to wave and smile before she got on the plane. I stood at the large windows of the waiting area until Claudine's plane glided down the distant runway and into the sky, until it grew tiny and disappeared. Suddenly I envied Roger Mosely, who had been so much more honest than I had been.

BOOKMARKS

Where is the page on which I found meaning
then lost my place,
the page with the turned corner,
soiled by so many readings,
oiled by a caressing hand
and sought again, like a loved one
whose train has left the depot too soon
and whose wave out an open window
grows a little dimmer in the distance?

Where are the words that, like flecks of shadow
from under some brilliant light,
persist across this snowy landscape of paper
in a pathway
to lead the wanderer home?

Where in this tome of chapters,
with their flashbacks and promises of resolution,
are the lines, only half remembered, that said
everything at once in perfect elegance,
like sun through veined leaves?

JB

Chapter 20 The "P" Word, or The Great Classroom Taboo

Miss Katherine Belle had just been hired as a permanent teacher for the English Department. She will always remain for me the absolute stereotype of the prim, no-nonsense, meticulous, tweedy old maid for whom a misplaced comma or dangling modifier could bring on a migraine. Like her personality, her hair was very stiff, as though it had been baked into an indestructible flip that could slice a loaf of stale bread. She wore heavy, mother-of pearl, rhinestone encrusted cat's eye-framed glasses from which hung a beaded chain that added drama to a powdered face, that was unremarkable, except for the lips, which against all reason and sense of balance, were a deep, ruby red, which made her look strangely like Dorothy Lamour in the early stages of becoming a Quaker. I didn't dislike her, but Miss Belle occasionally joined the rest of us at our usual lunch table and seemed to have no sense of humor at all. This made me worry about any success she might be able to achieve working with teenagers, whose lives were governed to a great extent by hormones and the rest by seeing the ridiculous all around them. It was also evident from those shared luncheons that Miss Belle did not even like teenagers. That impression made me want to set up a date between her and the infamous Jack Farrel, but I never actually did.

It was the year I would be receiving tenure, that archaic illusion of protection granted to those who had supposedly proven themselves capable of doing good work consistently. That first school day in September each year energized me, partly because of the shiny, newly-waxed floors and the smell of fresh paint, both of which continue to give me an enthusiasm for starting something new, or even just beginning again.

That was also the year that I designed plans for a creative writing class for seniors, plans that were accepted by the state of Indiana for an elective English credit. The course covered essays, short fiction and poetry. Poetry had always been one of the most interesting challenges in teaching English, because I knew that it was often taught badly, and what I wanted more than anything else was to publish every spring an anthology of student writing, including lots of poetry. I would like to address here some comments to those readers who are teachers of English and to anyone who has ever thought about writing any kind of poetry, and finally to those, who have been scarred along the way by poetry lessons based solely upon memorization or true-false quizzes.

At the risk of becoming too academic, I'd like to share some ideas that brought success to my students' initial attempts at composing their own poetry. This may be of interest to English teachers, but its message may find a place in hearts of many other people too. I base these ideas upon the premise that to appreciate more fully what poetry is and what it can be, writing one's own can give a far better perspective and understanding of the challenges and rewards of such writing. The same reasoning applies to painting, playing the piano, or playing basketball. We value any skills more, after attempting them and struggling to reach the payoff of being able to say, for example about a poem of some quality, however, short, "Yes, I wrote that."

There are certain words in our language that, for many students, are totally taboo. Poetry is one of these words. Its mere utterance in some classrooms can bring down an impenetrable curtain between students and teacher. The accumulation of impersonal, excessively academic experiences and cultural prejudices associated with poetry come into play. Mechanical study of the "great" poets tends to be, for many kids, remote and devoid of lasting influence, if there is no careful overture. Boys can have an especially difficult time with poetry if they are burdened by the misconception of poetry as a purely frivolous or strictly feminine pursuit.

For these reasons an introduction to poetry sets a precedent in attitude that can last for many years. It is possible to help students discover that they can generate real poetry by keeping in touch with their own experiences. It is also possible to convey the message that somebody can enjoy both baseball and poetry without being labeled schizophrenic.

Poetry is the most distilled form of language. It represents something large that the poet has packed neatly and efficiently into a smaller space. Rhyme is not a requirement, but when there is rhyme, it should not be more important than the poem itself. Teachers need to encourage experimentation and individuality in their students' efforts, making copies of their work (perhaps without names at first) available to the entire class, so that the poems can be read and discussed by everyone. This multiple feedback is excellent in aiding students to discover gradually the finest elements of poetry from the ground up. "Studying" the work of peers provides an immediacy far more effective for beginners than the experience of having a teacher impose "great" poetry. Once students write their own poetry and understand the challenge from inside the process itself, they begin to appreciate in more depth the work of other poets, including the "great" ones.

I usually began with figurative language and created some exercises to get students thinking about comparisons. Similes are a good beginning, showing that the comparison between two unlike things using the word "like" or "as" can yield something striking. For example, "The gray Persian cat fluttered over the sofa, like a puff of smoke." That comparison is based upon color and movement. A bowling ball wouldn't "flutter" over anything. Another example, this one by a six-year-old girl, is, "The sea made a sound like a silk dress." That simile is based upon the whispering sound made by a quiet sea and folds of silk brushing against one another. The best similes are striking because of their uniqueness and appropriateness. The simile, "As quiet as..." could not be completed skillfully with, "a mouse." Originality is essential for quality. It is simple to compose partial similes for students to complete. Here is a set I used to get my class started. Students were to complete each one with an original and striking ending:

1. The empty tire swing spun 'round, like...

2. Snowflakes lie on her black glove, like...

3. When the movie ended, the theater screen was a white as...

4. Beads of milk scattered over the floor, like...

5. The radiator exploded steam as evil as...

6. Leaping flames licked the upper windows, like...

7. Her face through the frosted window appeared like...

8. The voices and clanging locker doors made the school hallway sound much like...

9. The bare tree branches hung against the cold winter sky, like...

10. The glowing steel mill loomed, like...

I would then put students in groups of three or four to prepare more examples and present their efforts to the rest of the class, and we would discuss which ones worked best and why. The next step might be to use the similes as parts of actual poems composed by students themselves. Here are the first examples of my students' efforts using similes as the bases for short poems:

IDEAS

They melted into my mind, like
  Fannie May Mints,
disappearing into the core of my mouth,
seeping into my brain,
like plasma into the soul of a dying man,
they crept,
   They woke me,
    They shook me,
'Til I felt as though they would not stop.Then they loosened their tightness,
They led my mind on
through soft petals and fields,
dangling from above,
protruding from below,
filling the journey with delight.

They had achieved,

They had conveyed,
They had become.

Yvonne Wilson

The next figure of language might be metaphors, a comparison between two unlike things not using "like" or "as" but rather saying that one thing is something else, directly. If I say that, "Green leaves of jade hung in the Chinese garden," I have suggested that the tree leaves are jade, when, of course they are not, literally, but I have made a comparison anyway. The color green and the Asian reference provide enough association for the comparison to work. Another example might be, "The sun's gold was spent in ripples on the sea," the comparison being light and gold, color being the basis for the comparison through reference to sunset and to actual gold. Metaphors can be as rich or lean as one chooses and can, in fact, be set up almost like simple equations. Students may write a metaphor like, "The blackboard is licorice." At the heart of poetry is that almost magical ability human beings have for looking at at one thing and seeing something else. I had my students make lists of things upon which metaphors could be built. Clouds are an obvious example, because almost everyone has seen clouds as other things. A few early examples by my students of little poems based upon metaphor are:

Autumned valley,
Nature's patchwork of
amber, yellow, and
crimson trees.

Phil Markovich

THE FAN

It floats into a spectrum
of any colors you like,
and its far-reaching fingers
whisper
as it subtly unfolds its pages.

Over its horizon
are eyes which taunt you,
an object of flirtation,
which selflessly compliments.

Like the bound rope of hair
on an Indian maiden,
it captures uniform layers
of the feather which adorns her.

yet ever shyly it retires,
this man-made peacock,
and sweeps into its fluttering lashes
a tale of inner beauty.

Tina Douglas

EXIT

If we are over,
and the scene we set
faded,
the props now exactly that -
props,
Will you please go quietly
and bring down the curtain?
I will stay behind
and return the stage to order
and go on with the next act,
as if "we" never were.

Don't slam the stage door
as you leave.

Rhonda Sinsabaugh

A SCHOOL DAY

A school day is an everlasting
torment,
an overflow of the toilet of
education,
a sleeping pill that will kill you
if you sleep:
An overdose of confused words
a review of universal standard
encyclopedia,
a computer's memory consumed
in an hour,
and a hernia in the mind.

Harold Keutzer

Another catalyst for new poets is personification, another type of metaphor, assigning human characteristics to what are not humans. Something like a clock, for example, can be easily personified, since two characteristics shared by both humans and clocks are hands and faces. Here are a few short poems written by my students based upon personification:

HAIKU

Grasping the water,
the sun's radiant fingers
show their diamond rings

Sharon Jadrnak

THREE HAIKU

Sunflower stretches,
her fingers titling open,
nodding to the day

Soft downy meadow
the winds teach the wild flower
its free-form ballet

Seaside at midnight
becomes the looking glass for
a round summer moon

Tina Douglas

WHITE CAPS

The chef of the sea
gently mixes,
churns the cream,
then whips it
against the rocks.
Not satisfied,
he tries again.

Ron Rymarczyk

UNTITLED

Confusion in time
the hours slip by
with questions
dancing in my mind,
switching partners
in mass confusion.

Answers step in,
but the emotion
is too fast.

Penny Ellison

Finally, I introduced student poets to imagery, which is an appeal to one or more of the senses. The phrase, "burnt autumn leaves" evokes the sense of smell. Any word or phrase that can evoke the sense of sight, hearing, smell, taste or touch can vivify a poem by making a connection with the reader's physical experience. Even abstract words, like anger, hatred, and humor can take on fresh, concrete qualities in terms of imagery. Here are three examples by my students of poems based upon imagery:

ANGER

Its force tears at my soul:
Burning, red-hot branding irons
sear through me.

I hear the piercing sound of my alarm clock
drilling away at my ears,
or
the sound of a hundred sparking train wheels
scratching along the hard, iron tracks.
I see images of wild stallions rearing fiercely
or
flailing limbs of a tree
teased by the omnipotent wind.
Its fierce floods flow, bubbling
and churning between, over,
and slapping against huge rocks
that form themselves
within the moment's time.

Lori Davidson

HATRED

Hatred looks like a dark, stormy sky,
getting even darker with each disturbance.
It smells like tuna fish
left to thaw, but left too long.
Hatred tastes like cod liver oil
taken by the bottle.
It sounds like the explosion
made by an atom bomb.
Hatred feels like a bag
of broken glass,
sharp and cutting.

Scott Stevenson

HUMOR

Humor taste like a
lemon-flavored sweet tart.
It feels like a rubber ball
bouncing off a wall
and looks like a clown at a circus.
It smells like popcorn popping,
all fluffy and white
and sounds like a small child
watching Tom and Jerry.

Lisa Hunter

Making a list at the board, with help of students, of abstract words, like jealousy, freedom, sadness, fear, etc. can help stir up ideas for poems using imagery to make those words come to life in terms of the senses. As a beginning, ask how anger might taste.

Ideas for poetry don't always come on cue. Even great poets don't always summon poems based upon assignments. There is, however, a way to create a reservoir of material from which to draw ideas when needed. That is a journal, which for many has become a blog on computers. It can be a daily account of observations that accumulate over time, many of which we would forget if we didn't pin them down by writing them. Even a striped wash cloth draped over a bathtub may suggest a convict escaping Devil's Island. With practice, students can begin to see things all around them as fodder for later writing, seeing old things in new ways. Without observation, a day can be nothing more than blank space filling up time. It's no wonder that so many people complain about being bored if there's no loud music, cell phone, or computer activity pounding into their brains every moment of every day. They notice nothing, but with a journal of dated entries, like, "Today I noticed that the icicles over the garage looked like lead crystal and diamonds in the sun," one need never face a blank page for the creation of poetry. The journal will be a bank account of ideas that pay enormous interest later on, not only in poems, but in other kinds of writing too. In my creative writing classes, we wrote our own textbook as we went along, learning together through writing and discussion about that writing.

Meanwhile, our new faculty member, Miss Belle, was teaching the literature of England and considered "great poetry" of value to high school seniors, believing the works of poets like, Burns, Blake, Wordsworth, Coleridge, Keats, Shelley, Byron, and Browning worth studying, but she was very much against students writing their own poetry before they had a grounding in what she called the classics. "What do teenagers know about writing poetry anyway?" she asked. At our next two English Department meetings, Miss Belle ranted about what a complete waste of time it was to boost adolescent egos by making them believe they could create actual poetry or any other writing, except good, solid, formal essays. She then claimed my class was giving seniors a "fake sense of self-esteem," based upon the drivel I was encouraging them to create.

When I asked her how much of my students' poetry she had read, her only reply was, "Enough," while glaring at me through her rhinestone glasses, as though she might be starting a fire any minute. My arguments about the value of independent and creative thinking meant nothing to her. She remained as self-righteous as I did, but the difference was she was belittling my work, while I believed her work had importance of a different kind. Fortunately, two of my other department colleagues defended my methods by telling Miss Belle that poetry wasn't just an intellectual experience, but a sensory one. Glenn asked her why she was so determined to invalidate what students felt and thought. Not answering, she only sneered, turning away and then tucking her copy of THE WORKS OF TENNYSON tightly under her arm before exiting the room after the meeting was adjourned. Miss Lutt, a department colleague and old friend took me aside while we were collecting the remaining coffee cups and said, "You know, John, those seniors love your class, and it's just possible that your teaching poetry from the inside out instead of from the outside in is the best way, and that the prudish Miss Belle might be jealous of that success." I smiled at the comment, wanting very much to believe it was true, but my hope was to convince Katherine Belle that perhaps both our methods and goals for teaching had an important place in the educational scheme of things, and "scheme" became the operative word in all my further dealings with that bitter woman.

Chapter 21 Blame It All on the Wind

As sponsor of the Foreign Language Club, I arranged field trips to places like The Museum of Science and Industry in Chicago for events like the "Christmas Around the World" programs on Saturdays during the month of December. There were huge balsam trees decorated with ornaments from other countries across the globe, each tree representing a different nation with representative food and music. There were high school choirs from around the Chicago area singing yuletide songs from all over the world, songs that reverberated within those high stone walls, as though in some cathedral. I always chartered a school bus for these field trips, and we were back around four in the afternoon. There was a buddy system requiring students to explore in pairs or in groups with at least one person having a watch so that everyone could be at the front doors to catch the bus back at two. Only once did this method not work, and we left a girl at the museum. Her parents, fortunately, were on my side, as their daughter was notoriously late for everything at home as well, and parental threats over the years to leave her behind had come to nothing. Mr. and Mrs. Yeager saw this as a turning point in their daughter's upbringing. I'm not sure I'd be so lucky doing that today.

On one such excursion, as we were gathering together in the main lobby to exit for our bus, I saw a heavy-set woman with her five children. The lady was wearing a calico print cotton dress under an unbuttoned gray winter coat, but what caught my complete interest was that around her ample waist was a clothesline kind of rope to which were attached, at intervals, five other pieces of rope, each about four feet long, and each wrapped around the waist of a different young child. She and the children had almost the appearance of a single organism, like some impossible sea creature with appendages that moved independently, or a central sphere orbited by five satellites that managed to keep equal distances from the mother planet. I was so amazed by the sight, that my automatic reaction was to laugh out loud. Hearing me, the woman waddled over to the bench where I was sitting with some of my students, who had also noticed the strange sextet but were evidently too stunned even to register any reaction. Covering my mouth, and looking downward came just a bit too late, because the woman's indignation at my brief laughter zeroed in on me as the target for an angry lecture on parenting.

"Hey, you! Ya think this is funny?" she began.

"Not really," I answered.

"Well, you try keepin' five youngins together for even two minutes without a lasso, and see how YOU do."

"I'm sorry. I can't imagine," I said.

"You got kids?" she inquired.

"Yes, these are my kids," I lied, pointing to the four students, who were sitting with me on the bench.

After examining all four of them with her eyes, she said, "Well, they look old enough to look after theirselves. My kids is young, and this is just how I keep 'em safe. Ya got no right to be sittin' there titterin' away at us!"

"No, indeed," I ended.

Then she turned, jerking the ropes so that the children followed her, like the swirling hem of a big hoop skirt, and off they went.

Mortified by my own insensitivity, I looked at my students, who raised their eyebrows before bursting into fits of laughter, one boy actually doubled over on the floor, trying to catch his breath. The laughter continued on the bus most of the way home, the story making its rounds, seat by seat to those who had not been there to see my witless encounter with the mad woman, who would forever remain my most vivid memory of "Christmas Around the World."

Then there was our evening field trip to a French restaurant called the "Bon Appetit" in Crown Point, Indiana, an elegant Victorian mansion that had been purchased by a Parisian-trained chef named Louis, who made it the finest place to dine in Northwest Indiana. Foreign Language Club had another fundraiser, like the ones they had already had for trips to Mexican, Greek, German, and Thai restaurants. Twenty students, two parents, and three faculty members, including me, dined at the Bon Appetit on a Wednesday evening, enjoying a five-course dinner of exquisitely prepared French cuisine. A week before the dinner, I sent home permission slips on which parents could list any allergies their kids had, and I added that only with parental consent would a small glass of French wine be served with the entree.

The evening was splendid, mostly because of the superb food, but also because of the conversation, the private dining room we were given, with an enormous mahogany table and twenty-five various French antique chairs. The best part of the evening may have been the private tour Louis gave my students in French of the kitchen areas after the meal.

The next morning at school during my conference hour, I was called down to the office of Mr. Perkins, whose grave facial expression let me know even before I sat down that our meeting was not going to be a pleasant one. He told me about a phone chat he had endured with Mrs. Hanson, mother of Sharon Hanson, a Foreign Language Club member, who had attended the dinner the evening before. Apparently, Mrs. Hanson was extremely upset over her daughter's having had a glass of wine with her dinner. I remembered Mrs. Hanson from PTA meetings to which she had worn very low-cut blouses that emphasized a well-endowed frontage of Dolly Parton proportions. I sensed already a contradiction in this woman's package of values, but Mr. Perkins gave me her phone number saying simply, "Make things right with this woman." I was glad I had held on to the signed permission slips for future reference.

Phoning Mrs. Hanson, I began our conversation with an apology for any misunderstanding that might have occurred, and explained my confusion over the signed parental permission slip that Sharon had given me. There was a long pause before Mrs. Hanson continued, not with any comment on her daughter's having forged a signature, but rather with a mini-sermon on the fact that she and her family were active members in the Baptist Church under the divine guidance of Pastor Bowman. Hearing his name again made my heart sink at the instant thought of his next sermon becoming a diatribe against libertine teachers, who got their students drunk. It was another of those moments when I imagined a bad photo of me in the TIMES with a headline like, DEBAUCHED HIGH SCHOOL TEACHER TAKES STUDENTS ON HEDONISTIC BINGE."

Mrs. Hanson continued by assailing me with the arduous history of the "Christian training" her daughter had received against drinking, smoking, and sex before marriage. As soon as there was a slight opening in the dialogue, I injected the comment that it was especially surprising that having been taught so carefully all her life that alcohol was such a terrible vice, her daughter would forge a permission slip just for a little glass of red wine. There was another uncomfortable silence. My intention, of course, was to reveal a possible crack in Mrs. Hanson's puritanical instruction in order to help put the noose around Sharon's neck, where it belonged, not around mine.

I mean, it wasn't as though I had taken a bunch of kids to a back alley somehwhere, so we could all spend the evening chugging Jack Daniels or Jim Beam. In fact, I had given up my evening to show them a bit of culture to which they might not otherwise have ever been introduced. Later on, two or three other parents wrote me thank you notes expressing gratitude for my having given their kids an elegant and enjoyable evening of education they would never forget. It seems that one of Sharon's "friends" had spilled the beans to her own mother about Sharon's having had wine at the dinner, and that mother called Mrs. Hanson to let her know that sin was rampant.

The only other communication I received on the subject came from Pastor Bowman himself, who wrote a reprimand about my being guilty of "leading the young and innocent down dangerous paths of temptation." I composed several responses in varying degrees of outrage, none of which I actually mailed. It had become more than evident over my early years as a teacher, that trying to speak or write on any rational level with this pompous windbag was an utter waste of my energy and time.

There was always during those early years of teaching the issue of absences, along with the written excuses brought from home. My occasional visits to homes of questionable truants seemed to work fairly well in maintaining that greatest of all terrors, the mere possibility of a teacher going to anyone's house. I did, however, enjoy reading many of the notes that were on file from students in my homeroom, about half of whom had forged at least one excuse. Some of them were even typed to reduce the work of forgery down to only a signature. I'm pretty sure that in some of those notes, students had already reached some zenith of creativity, but it was the real notes from home, the notes written by parents themselves, that provided the most entertainment. I'll include just a few of the actual ones from parents:

1. Uncle Cecil came to visit, and he's a mean drunk. We were up all night making coffee, so Jimmy was absent yesterday. Mrs. Douglas

2. Please excuse Barbara for being absent yesterday. A thread from her only clean skirt caught on a doorknob and by the time I drove her to school, the thread was all over Hessville, and the skirt was unraveled up to her crotch. Mrs. Bertram

3. James was absent Wednesday, because he helped me clean the basement, where his daddy has to sleep. Mrs. Filmore

4. Barney was gone from school cuz we lost his Ritalin, and y'all don't want him in class without it. Mrs. Bradley

5. Dear teacher, Billy was absent Friday. A big raccoon got in the house.
Sincerely, Mrs. Blaskovich

6. Dear school, Cindy was gone from class for two days, because our new stereo system from Japan on volume ten blew out the picture window. Mrs. Fromm

My favorite three excuses for not turning in homework, two from the same girl, Denise, and one from a boy named Steve, were:

1. I didn't do the homework, because I had a problem with my eyes. I just couldn't SEE the point of writing all those sentences.

2. There's no percentage in it.

3. That wind this morning was sure strong, and just "tornadoed" the homework right out of my hands on the way to school.

It was prom time again, and I had been elected to serve on the faculty advisory committee, even though students made many of the final decisions about where the prom would be held, its theme, what the dinner would be, and what band would play. Though the theme would eventually be "Jamaican Holiday," I rather enjoyed going through the folded papers in the suggestions box to find everything from "Paris Under the Stars" to "Night of the Living Dead" as proposed prom themes. My favorite tardy excuse for the season for one of my senior boys was delivered by the kid on a piece of paper signed by the head secretary downstairs. It said just, "Tux problems. Joyce K"

It was still the era when on prom day, juniors and seniors were excused an hour early, mostly to permit the girls time in what for many must have proved to be a most rigorous session of primping and, for some, reclamation. It was always a fascinating mystery to me that prom night, especially for girls, was second in importance only to their wedding day. Reading fashion magazines for months and watching Oscar Night on television to see the gowns worn by stars, girls would defy sometimes cosmic forces to look as much like glamorous leading ladies as expensive cosmetics and Mother Nature would allow, but I was sympathetic, because prom was a rite of passage, particularly for the girls. The boys, I have always suspected, were all dressed in their tuxes and ready to go in less than thirty minutes, having spent the bulk of their time and effort cleaning and waxing the family car.

Prom night went well, except that one of the papier mache coconuts from one of the fake palm trees fell on Mr. Wagner's head and bounced off to knock over a fruit cup that stained a tablecloth.

It is surely a privilege for a teacher to be able to witness the lives of his students slowly becoming adults by their often stumbling through formative experiences, which certainly include learning about the United States Constitution, what a parabola is, and the three branches of American government, but I imagine that making touchdowns, home runs, debating with teachers and parents, going on their first dates, overcoming crushes, and marching down that long aisle to Elgar's Pomp and Circumstance #2 are all experiences that influence and form them as individuals along the way. No high school teacher can fail to be moved deeply by seeing kids he taught as freshmen receive diplomas before entering a world where all hopes and dreams will be tested, often much more harshly than in high school. It may be akin to that feeling parents have at the time they watch their kids leave the nest.

Chapter 22 Oh, Danny Boy

If I were giving advice to today's beginning teachers, I would tell them to find colleagues on the staff who shared their ideals and convictions, and I would ask them to share their concerns , hopes, and ideas. A teacher should never isolate himself, but be open to new ways of seeing. Such interest in life is fundamental to all learning and teaching. Personalizing one's teaching style helps develop his or her greatest gifts. Teachers need to accept that everyone is different, and to celebrate that diversity. No single, preconceived mold is ever good enough. Any teacher needs also to know that he won't reach everyone everyday in ways that are always traditional, but in the wider view, the teacher will be doing work that in its own way is changing the world. Every teacher has the awesome power to plant seeds, that can yield wondrous things that he may never even get to see, but the domino effects of teaching and learning are cosmic.

On the other hand, if I have given the impression that teaching is easy, that there are never battles of will with students, colleagues, administrators, and parents, that there are no days when feelings of failure creep about your desk through the seemingly unanswerable questions, "What am I doing here, and why am I doing it?" then I have not succeeded in giving a full picture of a marvelous profession that, like any other, has its days of glory and triumph, as well as its days of frustration and feelings of inefficacy. Anyone who thinks that teaching is little more than Miss Anna singing, "Getting to Know You" to the cheerful Siamese children, needs to rethink any hope of entering the profession.

Helping students to be able to read, understand, calculate, and to think critically and creatively is perhaps the most important but most unappreciated job on the planet. At Christmas there will be no monetary bonus or stock options, but rather a box of cookies, if you're lucky. Bright and talented people still enter the profession, but not for financial gain. The rewards they seek are more ethereal than ones that will purchase a yacht, or even a loaf of bread, and perhaps that's as it should be. There are many more brilliant people, who would certainly enter teaching if salaries were commensurate with those on Wall Street, but the dedication factor might disappear from the equation, where heart and love of one's work still trump motives based solely upon material profits.

None of this explains Danny Pinkerton, who like Johnny Madison was bright and even talented, but whose energy and purpose seemed devoted to creating a resistance movement more powerful than any other since the one in France during the German occupation of World War II. Thwarting any attempts to draw him into the fold of public education was his aim, and he was a master at it. After only four weeks, Danny had earned the faculty code name, "Spawn of Satan." Obviously, that was not the designation in Danny's school records. In his folder in the main office were many interesting pages of commentary by his teachers going back to kindergarten, some of the terms written with enough force to have dug right through the paper. The most striking words used to describe Danny were, recalcitrant, uncooperative, seemingly anti-social, indolent, unindustrious, and mean spirited. As in cases of past students, like Johnny Madison, I became thoroughly curious about Danny's background in school and wanted to meet the parents whom I pictured as Bonnie and Clyde.

Danny had been in my English class for only two weeks before using all the money in the book rental envelope to hire a professional hit man crossed my mind. Danny was less surly than he was inert, and there were days when he actually resembled a mannequin that someone with a diabolical sense of humor had simply dropped in that seat before running off to blow up a convent or Red Cross center. Though he had been issued a grammar and literature book, he never brought either to class, and I later found out that his mother had found them in her clothes dryer. Nor did Danny ever show up with pen and paper, though after class one morning, I did find an elaborate pencil rendering on his desk of "BOLINGER SUCKS." The florid lines suggested the style and skill of a medieval monk having lovingly inscribed an illuminated manuscript without the gilding.

Seeing all the trouble he had gone to in order to inscribe this not-exactly-Valentine message took me back to the venomous but artistic drawings of me that Johnny had done just a few years before, no real attempt to hide any angst, but rather to advertise it, yet in a relatively private way. I suppose it could have been much worse, as in the case a few years later when, over Christmas vacation, an angry and vindictive student on the staff of the school newspaper carefully tramped a huge message about the publications adviser in the snow on the football field that could be seen from all the second-floor windows facing south and probably from satellites overhead as well. "MR. MARTIN SUCKS" By comparison, this pencil drawing on a desk top seemed rather genteel.

In any case, every test paper, quiz, or composition Danny turned in had his name and the date in the upper right-hand corner, but the rest of each paper was always blank. I kept a folder for every student with all the essays and tests so that I'd have something concrete to show parents who might want to see samples of work that their children weren't bringing home. I knew that some contact had to be made with Danny's parents, and very soon. The longer I waited, the more difficult I knew things were going to be. None of Danny's other teachers had been in contact with his parents either, but they all confirmed that he was merely filling a seat daily and doing no work. His math and Spanish teachers told me they had never even heard Danny speak. My "talks" with Danny had yielded only responses of "I don't care" and casually shrugged shoulders that served only to confirm his few spoken words. The first two attempts at phoning his house got me busy signals. On the third try, Mrs. Pinkerton answered, but her voice was not loud enough to drown out the background noise of a television show called THE MATCH GAME, until I requested that she turn down the sound, which she did. Her gentle voice encouraged me to pursue a meeting in person with her and Mr. Pinkerton, to which she agreed, inviting me to their home the following evening, when she and her husband would both be at home.

Arriving at the Pinkerton house the next evening at exactly seven, I was invited to sit in a comfortable old chair that matched the rest of the very traditional furniture in a living room that could easily have served as a perfect stage set for Thornton Wilder's play, OUR TOWN, Norman Rockwell prints about the room, completing the mood of what appeared to be a stable environment, one that surely couldn't have produced someone as distant and contrary as Danny. One of the important lessons of teaching I learned over the years, however, was to expect the unexpected. The deep and abiding complexities of human nature are certainly the business of teaching, and I never ceased being astonished at the ironies of my own miscalculations and misinterpretations regarding people in my classes. That phenomenon made me less and less judgmental, and helped prepare me to accept the blue, spiked hair, tattoos, ear, nose, eye, tongue and lip piercings that would appear with some frequency during my later years as a teacher.

Mr. Pinkerton had the rough appearance of a blue collar worker, a man of burly, rugged, and gnarled visage and calloused hands. His wife, a delicate creature whom a breath might have withered, asked me if I'd like some coffee. Danny was still in his room, but would be joining us shortly when his dad called him. Before that, the three of us sat, as I listened to Mr. Pinkerton expound unemotionally about the harsh discipline that his son needed in order to become a responsible boy who, "does what he's supposed to do in class." I then asked if Danny did what he was supposed to do at home. His father looked at the floor for a moment before replying, "Yeah, but I have to bang him around a bit to keep him on track." Mrs. Pinkerton poured the coffee but said nothing. "That's the way my dad raised me, and I didn't turn out so bad," added Danny's father, with some forced laughter.

Danny entered the room and sat across from me, glaring at me in a way that let me know I was little more than an invader, a common interloping narc, come to spy on his private world. When I asked how he was, Danny's only response was, "Just fine." His laser stare continued as I nervously sipped the hot coffee.

"What do you want, Danny? What is it that makes you most happy?" I inquired.

"Nothin'," he answered, as his dad's right hand slapped the back of his son's head so hard, that Danny's whole body lurched forward, lifting him off his chair and also lifting his hair, which remained sticking up where the blow had struck. Still, Mrs. Pinkerton said nothing, as it became apparent that she had been well trained to defer to her bully of a husband in this and in all other matters, without comment or question.

Having spent an uncomfortable half hour there, I stood up to say that I had school work to complete and needed to leave. I thanked the Pinkertons for their hospitality and said that Danny still had the chance to receive a credit for his English course, and that I would do whatever I could to help. Danny sneered as I made my awkward exit, and his father's final words as I left were, "If my kid gives ya any lip or any other trouble, just let me know, and I'll beat the stuffin' outta him." Those words echoed in my head, even as I was falling asleep that night

My meeting with the Pinkertons helped me to understand whom Danny saw as the only boss of his life. His father was his only perception of authority, like some unsympathetic and vengeful god, waiting to strike him down if he failed to obey. Physical strength and force were Danny's comprehension of reasons for him to do anything. I began to see that, by contrast, I was some kind of weakling, who tried to use reason and abstract goals to persuade Danny to do his school work. He didn't, of course, recognize that my intention was actually to help him. Danny saw me, I believe, as only a feeble, impotent version of authority in his dad. I was only a paper cut-out of that brutal authority he was used to at home. My verbal attempts to get him through English class were powerless in Danny's eyes, partly because they were unaccompanied by the threat of fists or the weapon of a belt. He probably also felt empowered in his defiance of me. I suspect that, whatever else he felt for his mother, he had no real respect for her either. It may even be that in his eyes I was a carbon copy of her, someone whose lack of vocal volume and physical violence made her somehow unworthy of Danny's obedience and regard. That's exactly where I was in his eyes as well. It appeared that without a bat, I couldn't really get to first base.

Not wanting to tattle on Danny and have his face beaten in, I set about winning Danny's trust so that the rest of that semester he could still earn the credit he needed to point him toward eventual graduation and a diploma, that would also help keep his future options open. I couldn't tell if Danny had a sense of humor, but I was about to find out. Drollery had won over some former students, who were also angry and defiant, and I knew from experience that laughter could be a much stronger weapon than a threat, a fist or a belt.

There were days in all my classes, when some students would have their teenage periods of lethargy, those times when the meaning gets sucked out of everything, and kids want only to lounge on a sofa somewhere, eating Oreos and watching GILLIGAN'S ISLAND. Hands in class would not rise enthusiastically on those days to answer questions or join in discussions. It was on one of those lazier-than-usual afternoons that I resolved to try something totally but necessarily outrageous to win back some of the waning zeal of my classes.

Someone had brought to school a mannequin's head and blond wig from her uncle's department store. It had been used for a taped skit in one of my French classes and then tossed into one of the storage cabinets at the back of my classroom. During my conference hour the next day, I stacked about two feet of books on a desk chair in the front row facing my lectern and desk. I put a big sweatshirt over the books, stuffing the arms with wads of newspaper and cotton. Filling the sweatpants with more paper and cotton, I pinned the bottom hem to an old pair of basketball shoes on the floor, making the body begin to take shape. I sewed stuffed garden gloves to the ends of the sweatshirt sleeves, then placing the wigged mannequin's head on top of the stack of books that served as the torso. The head was at the neck opening of the shirt, and I wrapped a winter muffler around the opening, which gave the new student a sporty look. The whole thing looked kind of freaky, but she did resemble a real person, especially from the classroom door at the back of the room, where one could see this creature only from behind, her blond hair flowing around her square shoulders.

To give life to the "new student," I tied fishing line around her right wrist, hoisting the line through a bent paperclip on one of the metal supports for the ceiling tiles over her desk, the end of the line attached to a convenient handle at my own desk. The stage was set, and I could hardly wait for Danny's English class, who after the next passing bell began to trickle into the room, chatting and moving to their own seats, but every one of the students caught by the strange sight of the stationary body in front of the class. It was all I could do not to burst into uncontrollable laughter, as one by one, students walked up to that desk to examine the apparition. Each bent down a little to look at the face before exploding into every level of hilarity, from quiet chuckles to unabashed guffaws. Then, of course, all eyes were on me, the obvious and deranged perpetrator of this jest, so I moved to the front of the room in order to take roll and to introduce our new student, Miss Blanche Poodink from Hackensack, New Jersey.

"Please help to make Blanche feel at home," I pleaded.

One boy asked, "And what kind of HOME would that be, Mr. Bolinger?"

There was more laughter, though Danny just sat there with his usual steely, clenched jaw, no sign of emotional reaction.

I began the lesson, which was based upon using the new list of vocabulary words from A TALE OF TWO CITIES in original sentences, which could be goofy, as long as the words fit through use of the correct parts of speech. A few hands went up for the first word, but I felt greedy to have more participation, so I called on Danny, something I hadn't done for more than a week. He didn't move or blink, or even show that he was breathing. This was the moment. Standing at my desk, I pulled the fishing line, and Blanche's right hand rose in a ghostly response. One girl screamed, and several others in the room jumped in shock at seeing what they had deduced was a dead prop suddenly come to life.

"Well, " I said. "It appears that Blanche here is more alive than some of the rest of you. If a dummy can raise her hand, surely the rest of you can too, and the huge advantage you all have over her is that you have brains and voices. Poor Blanche means well, but she's mute." Though I could tell Danny was fighting it, a corner of his mouth moved slightly, gradually growing into the first smile I had seen from him. Then, he laid his head on his desk, shaking with laughter. It was a beginning.

Blanche stayed in that desk the rest of that year and was blamed for all sorts of classroom shenanigans. "Blanche did it" became the sentence that each of us used, including me, though Blanche did always receive an "A" in conduct. Our only problem with Blanche came one night, when Mrs. Johnson, a new custodian, entered my classroom to wash the boards and to mop up. Turning on the lights and seeing Blanche's back and flowing blond hair perfectly still and silent, Mrs. J, according to stories circulated by the other janitors on night duty, actually fainted and was found, mop-in-hand, at the entrance to my classroom, recovering later, only after being taken to the Blue Bird Tap on Kennedy Avenue, where she drank three shots of whiskey and smoked a whole pack of Camels.

Chapter 23 "My Teeth Itch"

Danny Pinkerton had as much right to be rebellious as any other student I ever knew. The brutal and unsympathetic authority of his father was enough to create a factory conveyor belt of angst on Danny's part, that led straight to school and into my classroom, where no physical violence would be practiced, but where Danny could express his anger at and defiance of his father with consequences that were generally in a state of postponement. Not able to lash out physically at his dad, Danny made school his scapegoat as a means of indirectly opposing that nemesis at home, even at the cost of being verbally and physically abused later on.

As in other cases where kids were exploding with rage that needed some relatively safe outlet, I gave Danny a spiral-ringed notebook for which I asked him to provide any title he wished, and to write whatever he wanted to write on any subject, without fear of censorship. Danny had a lot to say, a lot that he had never been allowed to say. My hope was that the notebook would be a secure place to release his fury. He needed badly to vent. I also suggested that he keep the notebook in a place, where no one else would be able to read it without his permission. He looked at me for a long time in a way that seemed to be waiting for me to say, "I was only joking." When I told him I was perfectly serious and that it might be a good way out while getting writing practice, he looked at me again as though I were some bizarre exhibit behind glass at a carnival, before asking, "Can I draw in it sometimes too?" I answered, "You may," and he smiled.

Miss Belle continued to offer her halfhearted smile, whenever we encountered each other at faculty meetings, in the halls, or in the cafeteria. Her stiff, unyielding appearance spoke volumes on her views of education and on life itself. Her sense of convention was indissoluble, and it was always apparent that she saw me as some kind of upstart, whose teaching methods were too liberal and unconventional to be tolerated.

After the school's first issue of EQUINOX, a sixty-page, eight-by-ten literary magazine of the best prose, poetry, and art work from the student body, I placed copies in the mailboxes of several on the faculty, including Miss Belle. In my mailbox the following morning were from all teachers whom I had given copies notes of praise and thanks, all except Katherine Belle, who had put her copy back into my mailbox, without comment. It was all I needed to know, exactly how she felt about the book and all the effort students had put into its creation. Her snub was not enough, however, to reduce my feelings of pride at producing something filled with the creative efforts of our students, something that encouraged writing, and something that would become a precedent for my remaining twenty-four years of teaching.

I should inject here a word about classroom emergencies, things with which over my thirty-five years in the profession I had little experience, fortunately. My mentor Miss Mason, who retired in 1970 after forty-four years as a teacher, had many stories to relate, including a knife-fight between two sophomores in the 1950's, and a girl's water breaking during a pop-quiz over THE LAST OF THE MOHICANS. Nothing so grand as either of those incidents ever occurred in my classroom, but there were minor episodes along the way worth noting, only for their frequency and occasional humor.

One incident involved Larry Zardock, a student in my sophomore homeroom, who was hovering around my desk one morning, and for no apparent reason, put his right hand inside the stapler, and before I could stop him, leaned down with all his weight. Then pulling his hand out, he looked intently at his forefinger, which had a staple going in one side and coming out the other. His eyes crossed in complete concentration at what at first must have seemed an optical illusion, before looking at me to say, "I think I need to see the nurse." Surprisingly, there was only a slight trickle of blood, probably because the staple was still blocking any free flow from the wound. I wrote him a pass to the nurse with a big question mark as my only explanation, and he appeared the next day with a bandaged finger, and nothing further was ever said on the subject, though I did wonder what story he took home to his parents.

Another accident occurred after school one day, when several students were in my classroom editing items for our next issue of EQUINOX, using a paper cutter and scissors to trim typed entries for layout. Nowadays, of course, computers make layout so much safer, but in those days, editors faced the primitive dangers of sharp tools of the trade. It would seem to people in the "outside world," or as we teachers used to call it, "the real world," that in kindergarten and other elementary classes, a teacher would have to take extreme care to monitor any use of even plastic, round-tipped scissors in the hands of their young charges. Perhaps I was yet naive in my faulty assumption that juniors and seniors in high school could use actual scissors without any real danger. Silly me! Matt Hampton, an otherwise mature and intelligent fellow, surprised us all that afternoon by cutting through a piece of paper and his finger at the same time with his scissors, creating a wound large enough to allow a disturbing flow of red that made one of the girls scream, "Oh my God!" My wrapping a handkerchief tightly around the base of his finger decreased the flow, but Matt still left a trail of blood on our entire trip down to the nurse's office, his arm held up the whole way to further stem the flow.

Mrs. Baker created an excellent bandage for the cut and told Matt to keep his right arm elevated for a while. I drove him and the other students home, Matt's arm held up and outside the front passenger window all the way. Mrs. Hampton seemed grateful for my care of her wounded son, but commented that she might expect such a thing to happen during football practice or in wood shop, but not while editing a magazine. I only smiled awkwardly before leaving. The lesson affirmed again and again over the coming years of teaching that when a teenager is distracted, grave dangers can lurk in the darkest corners of possibility. Almost incredibly, that broken concentration, brief as it may be, can mean the kid can hurt himself, even with a bag of marshmallows, if he's too near a flame. The lesson for me ever after remained that I would always be vigilant of any possibility that my high school students could injure themselves with anything from a rubber band to a ball point pen.

Some teenagers have an arsenal of excuses to leave a classroom in order to use the rest room or to see the school nurse, whose office was full of comfy chairs. My favorite request for exoneration from current class work via a trip to Nurse Baker, came from a freshman named Troy, who raised his hand in a panic during a spelling lesson and said in a voice filled with hysteria, "Mr. Bolinger, my teeth itch!" Suddenly all eyes in the room were upon him, as if he had become the main attraction of a traveling freak show. I tried to explain to him that teeth couldn't itch and that what he felt was only an illusion, and that the nurse would not be able to help, but for the rest of class he continued scratching his front teeth with a pencil eraser.

The strangest exit from my class to see the nurse came from my urging, not the student's. A sensitive and intelligent junior, Ben seemed one afternoon in my American Literature class to have lost all connection with his surroundings, not responding to my having called on him twice, and not even looking up from what he was reading at his desk. Walking back to where he was sitting, I tapped him on the shoulder, which startled the poor boy, so that he jumped up, as though he had not been aware of my presence in the room. It seems that during lunch that day, Ben had become annoyed enough by the cafeteria noise to place pieces of a chicken nugget into both ears. Apparently, the chicken plugs worked beautifully to eliminate sound but were lodged deeply enough in each ear canal to require the nurse's help with tweezers and cotton swabs to remove them later that afternoon.

Incidentally, that was the same year that I saved a chicken nugget from the school cafeteria in early October, keeping it until the last day of school in June. The nugget stayed dutifully on the top shelf of the bookcase behind my desk, untouched all those months until after final exams, when students in one of my French classes asked to witness the result of the eight-month experiment. The nugget looked just as it had looked all those months before, the bread crumb coating the same toasty, brown it had always been. Though slightly lighter in weight, due perhaps to some loss of moisture, the piece of chicken remained visually in tact, even after I threw it at a bulletin board across the room, the nugget bouncing, like a little rubber ball. Aside from the rather humorous and unexpected outcome, I'm not sure there was any real lesson for students on the sometimes frightening effects of food preservatives, but we laughed ourselves silly, and it was a good way to end the school year. Who says that science and French can't mix?

That summer I spent preparing for the Purdue University final exams leading to my Master of Arts degree in English Literature and Linguistics. Though ultimately more difficult than the Master of Science in Education, my degree freed me from the terminally dull courses in pedagogical theory, which were generally trendy explorations of demeaning value. The M.A required that I read copious numbers of the great books in our language, including novels, plays, essays, and poetry. Though my specialty was to be English Literature of the 18th Century, something I would undoubtedly not be using in teaching high school, I felt enriched personally by the knowledge it gave me and the reinforced joy in literature that would always serve me well in teaching.

Because that summer of 1977 was especially hot and humid in Northwest Indiana, I closed myself up with the air conditioning on, generously supplied with iced tea and lemons, surrounded by mountains of books from the classes I had been taking the previous several years from BEOWULF to Virginia Woolf. I devoured and inhaled it all again during the sixteen-hour days, cloistered, like a Trappist monk with his books, parchment paper, and quill pens. I had no television, but listened to classical music on Chicago's WFMT station of my 1955 Zenith mahogany radio, switching sometimes to playing LP recordings on my stereo, occasionally astonished at how well Carole King and Elton John complemented Chaucer or Jane Austen.

My little apartment became a time capsule during those months, taking me back to John Donne, William Shakespeare, Alexander Pope, Charles Dickens, D. H. Lawrence, and Dylan

Thomas, among others, much of my reading punctuated by music of James Taylor, Seals and Crofts, and The Doobie Brothers. Taking only two weekends off to join friends at their cottage at Lake Hudson, I spent that summer as a hermit among my books and papers, as happy as I had ever been or ever would be again, passing with high marks the exams that earned me the Master of Arts degree.

When September came yet again, I felt anxious to leave behind the world of being a student in favor of being a teacher again in the only place I knew, where someone's teeth could itch, where creative excuses for not doing homework flowed like honey, and where I actually felt needed.

Chapter 24 "Look out! Here Comes the Gerbil Again!"

The private journal seemed to be working for Danny, who allowed me to read entries that fully and honestly described his anger at being treated like a wayward child by his insensitive and demanding father, who was more a bully than a parent. Danny's mother seemed also to be a mere pawn on her husband's chess board, a woman who probably wanted deeply to help her son, but had neither the physical stamina, nor the endurance of will to contradict Mr. Pinkerton.

I must admit that it was gratifying to know that Danny was thinking things through in terms of his own future and what success in school might mean in helping him escape the tyranny of life at home. His journal was sometimes painful to read, because he wrote so clearly and effectively in recounting his experiences of being treated so often like a trained pet at home. The drawings accompanying his descriptive disclosures of home life were mostly renderings of an apartment he imagined having after leaving his parents' house. Though I didn't go into detail about Danny's progress, I did write a letter to his folks, letting them know that he was doing his assignments and was doing well. I never mentioned the journal.

A new student from Chicago arrived one morning with her counselor to be placed in my freshman English class. Her name was Trudy Butler, an overweight girl of long blond hair with black roots and wearing a gray corduroy skirt and white cotton blouse, neither of which fit her overly ample proportions. As always, when all other eyes in the room landed on her in the most critical ways, my heart went out to her, because as someone whose own family had moved several times while I was in school, I remembered what it was like to enter a new classroom filled with staring eyes judging every step I took. It was obvious how uncomfortable Trudy felt on that seemingly endless journey to the front of the room, where I introduced her before leading her to the psychological safety of a desk in the back row, where she could be the one to look at everyone else for a while, safe from the gaze of all except those who had to do some neck stretching and back twisting to put Trudy on display again.

After class I told her that if she encountered any problems, she should let me know. New students often needed all the help they could get, so I always felt protective of them, especially during those first few weeks when they were getting their wings.

Meanwhile, Principal Perkins was preparing to leave his job as head administrator of our school. In fact, he was being booted out, due to his ineptitude as our leader and placed in the curriculum department downtown at the board of education, where he could do little harm and prevent the possibility that higher powers might have to fire him, thus admitting having been mistaken in hiring him in the first place. There were students, who seeing Mr. Perkins as late as May or even early June, were still asking who he was, this man who was seen in public even less often than the reclusive Greta Garbo.

Our new principal was to be Mr. Jeremy Kelton, a former business manager for the Hammond Schools and for a company in Chicago, someone judged by the powers that be for his expertise in business management skills, which were, according to those powers, the greatest qualifications anyone could possess in running a school. It would prove to be more of the same old story, one that I'm sure is quite common in other public schools across the country, that the most important gift for any school administrative job was that someone could balance the financial books, not be a community figure of intelligence, diplomacy, dynamic academic experience, or sensitive and respected leader of both teachers and students.

Like Mr. Perkins, Jeremy Kelton never bothered to learn names of most on the faculty, except those of the coaches of sports. His two passions were our winning football games and our spending less money on books and supplies, at least in the academic wing. The man's interest in academics was, in fact, nil.

His respect and devotion were reserved for coaches of what he believed were truly essential parts of public schools, competitive sports. This good-old-boy club were the recipients of funding and moral support from the administration in a system, the hierarchy of which began with Mr. Kelton and Mr. Poteja, who seemed to enjoy excluding academics from school life. Public participation in and support of games on the football field, basketball court, or baseball and soccer fields were of tremendous value, according to Mr. Kelton, because of the importance of public relations and the enthusiasm that sports generated in the media. French, geometry, and biology didn't have that kind of popular or community presence. Ergo, we in academics were pretty much on our own.

One windy morning after parking in the front faculty lot, I saw Mr. Kelton walking quickly toward the front doors of the school and through the small groups of students already gathered and waiting for the first bell. That area around the front of the building was always a wind tunnel with bunches of leaves often swirling up in miniature funnels before being blown through the big red doors and into the school's foyer. That morning, however, there was to be something else joining those little leaf tornadoes. I heard a boy yell, "Look out! Here comes the gerbil again!" As my eyes wandered around the parking lot, I didn't see anything at first and thought the gerbil reference might be to a cluster of the spinning leaves. What I saw next came as an amusing, if not shocking, surprise. Mr. Kelton's toupee was flapping on his head like some anxious bird taking off from the precarious ledge of a cliff. Then it simply took flight as Mr. Kelton's hand, arriving too late to stop the toupee's escape, made a smacking sound on his bald head. Then twisting and turning in the wind, the hair piece continued its way across the parking lot until a senior boy stepped on it, halting its brief but exciting journey. Then walking over to the red-faced principal, the boy presented to him the toupee, like some exotic little creature brought back as a rare gift from a safari.

Apparently something like this had happened before, perhaps several times in order for the flying toupee to have acquired the nickname of, "The Gerbil." Not arranging the toupee on his head, Mr. Kelton just slipped it into his coat pocket before entering the building, the door closing behind him before the entire parking lot exploded in unbridled laughter, though I managed to hold it in until reaching my classroom, running all the way to my desk, where I laughed so hard, there were tear stains on the front of my shirt until second period.

During homeroom on every day there was to be a football game, Mr. Kelton would come on the P.A box to scream his message of, "Go get 'em, Govs!" Then he would play the sound track theme from the film, ROCKY so loudly, that the wall speakers would shake. There was no escape, and even students, after hearing this on so many occasions, began covering their ears with everything but chicken nuggets to avoid the forced and blaring dispatch from our principal. For that reason, I never felt the slightest bit of guilt at having laughed myself almost unconscious over the flying toupee incident. Our dignity as "The Governors" had been compromised by this Philistine on almost a daily basis.

After a few weeks, it was announced that Mr. Kelton was going to marry one of the counselors, Miss Beverly Adams, and that the wedding would take place on the Friday of homecoming in the cafeteria commons area after lunch. Faculty, who were free that hour were invited to stop by for cake and coffee. The wedding colors were to be red and gray, the school's colors, which would be worn by the bride and groom on a special float made in their honor for the parade before the game that evening.

All of this confirmed my earlier view that Mr. Kelton was a vulgar man, but I had no idea how far he could actually sink into creating a new definition for the word, "crass," making his marriage to Miss Adams part of the homecoming festivities, that would include his bride, a woman for whom I had great respect, until I saw her dressed in a gray taffeta gown with a red veil and gloves and red satin shoes. My only hope was that the marriage would not be consummated on their float as it drove majestically down Kennedy Avenue that evening, giving Mr. Kelton the ultimate sports PR he craved so much. In any case, homecoming would never again be the same.

My new student, Trudy Butler, had found a small group of other girls, who took her under their wing so that, like most other students, she found security in being part of a social segment of her class. It always eased my mind to see a new student find that special niche of social acceptance among peers, that little caravan of protection that offered their approval through friendship, embracing an often frightened newcomer, who needed no longer feel like a stranger in a strange land.

Danny Pinkerton went through three spiral-ring notebooks in the time he was in my class, received his English credits from me for freshman year, and even after moving on to the sophomore English class of another teacher, continued sharing with me journal entries that he refused to show anyone else. Because his grades had improved so much, and his parents were receiving very positive messages from all his teachers, Danny's journal entries became less angry, even though he continued to write that he felt strong enough to endure whatever time he might have left at home before finding happiness on his own.

The Pinkertons even invited me over for dinner, where I had the chance to praise their son, telling them they could be completely proud of him. One of the final entries in Danny's journal spoke of his having been in a state of "suspended animation" because of his father, but that as Danny felt more and more confident in his own skin and in his own abilities, his life had become more an "animated suspension," that would become even more alive when he was able to leave home eventually.

Frank Purcell, one of my American Literature students from the year before was then a senior in Miss Belle's English Literature class, in which they were currently reading Christopher Marlowe's DR. FAUSTUS, a play filled with wonder and profound questions on the human situation. Frank told me that Miss Belle's lectures were very well organized but extremely dry, as though she knew the work well but felt nothing of its excitement or terror. Remaining aloof at this piece of news, I was also not surprised to hear that Frank had offered Miss Belle a copy of the previous year's issue of EQUINOX, the same issue she had returned to my mailbox without comment. He had wanted her to read the two poems of his which had been published in the book, poems that for a high school junior had been quite good in their use of imagery and design. He then told me that having received a copy, Miss Belle looked sternly at Frank before handing the book right back to him with the comment, "Frank, I'm not interested in reading anything from this tabloid of student writing, and I suggest that you spend your time reading some real poetry from your English Literature text book."

Still visibly shaken by the woman's colossal snobbery and insensitivity, Frank could only look down at the magazine he had just placed on my desk. I told him not to take her criticism seriously, as she had not even bothered to read anything in the book. After Frank left, I squeezed my hands together so tightly, that they made a cracking sound, and I knew in that moment that there was going to be a serious confrontation between me and the imperious, egotistical Miss Belle.

Chapter 25 The Japanese Connection

Miss Belle and I had the same conference hour, when there would be no students to witness whatever confrontation or face-off she and I would be having, not excluding a possible homicide. After the bell rang for that period to begin, I started my walk down the long, empty corridor of highly waxed tile floors toward her classroom, stopping twice at drinking fountains, not because I was thirsty, but because I was very close to losing my nerve. It was important to me that I vent some of my accumulated frustration about Miss Belle to her face, not in a letter, which I had considered briefly as a way of expressing my dismay at her most recent, callous behavior. Reaching her door, I knocked before going in, taking a deep breath, as though preparing to enter the bone-cracking cold of an arctic storm.

Her glasses halfway down her nose, Miss Belle looked up from a paper she was grading, an expression of utter surprise and contempt on her face as I stood in the doorway, like an uninvited guest, or a salesman with a sack of Bibles to show an atheist. She asked me in and offered a conference chair facing her desk.

"Well, well! To what do I owe the honor of this unexpected visit?" she began.

"I'm not sure it will prove to be an honor," I said, "but I need to talk with you about a former student of mine, whose feelings you intentionally or unintentionally shredded yesterday after school."

"Oh? I'm certain that any wound I may have caused was not intended, but please tell me about it." she continued.

"For me, Katherine, this is an issue of huge importance, because our students are more sensitive and vulnerable than we ever give them credit for," I said.

"I'm all ears," she injected, smiling slyly.

"My primary concern right now is the very negative reinforcement you're conveying to students about their writing, writing that you haven't even bothered to read."

There was a long pause, as she looked hard at me, folding her hands before her, almost as though she were going to pray.

"Look, John, you don't seem to realize that high school kids aren't capable of any quality writing, especially poetry, and yet you continue to boost their egos with the preposterous notion that they're poets. You're doing them a terrible disservice," she asserted.

"How many of their poems have you actually read?" I asked.

"None, I'm happy to say," she replied.

“Ah!” I said. “That says it all and explains not only your insufferable snobbery, but also the basic prejudices of your closed mind. When a student comes to you in good faith, offering you samples of his writing in a publication he presents as a gift, and you reject it, telling him he should be reading ‘real poetry’ from a textbook, you are beneath contempt.”

“I was only being honest with him,” she continued.

“No!” I added. “You were rude to a sensitive, intelligent kid who sought your good opinion. Don’t you realize, woman, how many of these kids get absolutely no encouragement at home, and how reassuring and important a little word of comfort or praise from us can be?”

“I won’t lie to him, as you do” she blurted.

“You didn’t even look at his work, and even rejected the gift of the book itself. It’s time you stopped grandstanding for Lord Byron and started being a teacher, who cares about her students more than the rhyme scheme of a Shakespearean sonnet!” My voice had increased in volume more than I had intended.

“I believe I’ve heard quite enough,” she concluded.

“Not NEARLY,” I replied, “but for the moment I’ve finished. If your own heart had any tenderness or feeling, you might actually write some poetry yourself! Good afternoon.”

I didn’t slam the door on my way out but closed it softly behind me and stood in the empty hallway, my eyes closed and my heart beating like a hummingbird’s. Had I done the right thing, or had I just made things a lot worse for kids in her classes? As I walked back to my own classroom, I wondered how things might have turned out for the teenagers, Shelley and Keats, had they been students in Miss Belle’s classes. The poor guys might have become coal miners instead of great poets.

A year passed, and it was again October, almost time for homecoming. Miss Belle and I had not spoken to each other since our verbal exchange the previous year but managed through sheer determination to avoid hand-to-hand combat at faculty and PTA meetings. Neither of us seemed capable or even willing to edge toward the other’s point of view, so a silent truce remained in place between us not to argue or throw any blunt objects.

It was announced at a faculty meeting in mid-October that during homecoming week, our school would be hosting a team of sixteen high school teachers from Tokyo, Japan, teachers who had been chosen to do a group study of public education in The United States. Hoping for some good publicity, Mr. Kelton had volunteered our school as one of the sites for study and made arrangements for accommodations for the visiting teachers, most of whom taught science and math in and around Tokyo. The leader of their group had studied at the University of Paris, so he spoke French. His name was Akio, and he was six feet-six inches, the tallest Japanese person I had ever seen. The others in his group often hovered around him, like baby chicks around a mother hen, or Lilliputians around Gulliver. A great surprise to me was that no one in the group really spoke English, or at least no one admitted having that skill, not even Akio, whose name in English meant, “glorious hero.”

When the team of teachers arrived at Morton, there was already a tight itinerary in place for them to observe our school and community life, but when it was discovered how little English the group knew, Mr. Kelton assigned me the task of being the group's guide for the week, only because Akio knew French, which became the vehicle of understanding. I would speak French to Akio, who would then translate into Japanese for his group, and their Japanese was filtered through French for me to translate back into English for our faculty and students. The whole process seemed like an unnecessary language meat grinder, but it worked, slow and cumbersome as it was.

With Akio's help, I made a sheet of common English phrases and sentences with their Japanese equivalents, copies made available to the whole school. It's very likely that our dubious Japanese pronunciation altered the meanings of some of those phrases, though I'll never know how badly, but there were sometimes raised eyebrows and half-smiles on the faces of the Japanese teachers, who were otherwise the essence of humility and politeness, bowing frequently during any encounters with each other or the rest of us. I'll include part of that list of English phrases with their phonetic counterparts for anyone who may be interested in learning a little bit of Japanese:

English Greetings:	JapaneseGreetings:
Hi!	Yaa!
Good morning!	Ohayougozaimasu.
Good evening!	Konban
Welcome!(to greet someone)	Youkosoirasshaimashita.
How are you?	Ogenkidesuka?
I'm fine,thanks!	Watashiwagenkidesu.
And you?	Anatawa?
Good/So-So.	Genkidesu./maa-maadesu.
Thankyou(verymuch)!	Arigatou!
You're welcome!(for"thankyou")	Douitashimashite.
I missed you somuch!	Samishikattadesu.
What'snew?	Saikindoudesuka?
Goodnight!	Oyasuminasai.

See you later!	Mataatodeaimashou!
Goodbye!	Sayonara!

I was interested to learn how aware Japanese people were of the meanings of their own first names. Some of the men's names were Katsu (victory), Masaki (flourishing tree), and Takumi (adroit artisan). The women's names I liked even more, Akira (bright, clear), Haruki (springtime tree), Midori (green, verdant), and Mizuki (beautiful moon). Their names were the stuff of poetry, and I loved hearing them.

The team sometimes traveled as one group around the building, but more often, they visited classes in pairs, so as not to crowd the rooms they were observing. Though their stopovers in classrooms were regarded with great interest by our students and faculty, our guests taking careful and copious notes in each room, there was always the question of how much they were able to glean, not knowing our language. Akio told me that there was assiduous attention given to rapport in each class between teacher and students, as well as to responsiveness and level of excitement in every class.

I and some other members on our faculty thought the timing of the visit unfortunate, as homecoming week was certainly not representative of the usual academic atmosphere seen the rest of the school year. It had been Mr. Kelton's hope to show the Japanese team the most dazzling sample of our school year, complete with P.A. interruptions intended to arouse team spirit for the homecoming football game on Friday evening, pep rallies, a homecoming queen assembly, and daily playing of the theme from ROCKY during homeroom. This circus atmosphere worried some of us, who believed that these people from the most rigorous educational system on earth might not be able to take us seriously if they thought that homecoming week was just business as usual.

I also resented having a substitute teacher taking my classes part of that week, so that I could accompany Akio and his team around the building and on a one-day tour of Hammond. Happy to have my classes back by Friday, I still accompanied the Tokyo team to the homecoming assembly Friday morning, watching the astonished looks on their faces during the loud program and during the even louder pep session in the gym. I told Akio to explain to his group of teachers that all this silliness they had witnessed during the week was not at all typical of American public school activity, and that sports were not as pervasive as the team might have come to believe. The giggles and whispers, however, during each successive demonstration of American buffoonery on that Friday convinced me that whatever written reports were submitted to Tokyo, they would make Morton High School a global laughingstock.

The last part of the afternoon that Friday was spent by the Tokyo teachers walking through the school to observe one last time the classes that were in session. When the team congregated outside my classroom, a few cupping their hands to get a better view as they peered through those hallway windows to examine the climate of eagerness in my class at week's end, I went into a mild state of panic. It was my basic English class and the last period of the day on Friday, when most ardor for school work had waned to a thin vapor.

Knowing that the Japanese teachers understood almost no English, I decided to perk up my class in those final minutes before the bell rang by asking, "Well, how many of you would like to go home a little early today?" I know it was a sneaky trick, but all hands in the room shot up instantly, some kids practically leaping from their seats at the adrenaline rush that question had just given them. Our Japanese guests smiled broadly at each other, nodding their deep approval as they continued down the hallway to the next room. I waited until they were out of sight before dismissing my class three minutes early, wanting to honor my earlier insinuation of allowing them all to leave ahead of time. Then I breathed a sigh of relief at the thought that the foreign guests might remember my zealous students' hunger for knowledge, even late on a Friday afternoon, that could possibly blot out part of the recollection of the homecoming queen assembly swimsuit competition.

The Japanese teachers attended the football game that evening, which we won, as is usually the case for the home team, especially when the opposing team couldn't have played any worse, had they been from the Shady Pines Nursing Home, using walkers. On Saturday evening, our faculty hosting committee took the Tokyo team to dinner at Holiday Inn, where our Japanese guests sang us some of their country's folk songs and taught us some Japanese dances. The cocktails flowed, like tsunamis, until later in the evening, when there were a few of our Tokyo friends dancing on tables and making headpieces out of their linen napkins. It was truly amazing to see this transformation of meek and reserved Japanese citizens into the wildest partiers I had seen since college, but I think that's the very explanation. The strict and very demanding lives they led as the world's most formidable educators simply fell apart after a couple of martinis, and turned them temporarily into Americans! Sayonara, my friends.

Chapter 26 Unsung Heroes

I'm sorry to say that the conflict between Miss Belle and me never found resolution. We were never uncivil to each other, and perhaps we both lived on the edge of further attempts to bring about an amicable and mutual respect, but instead, we continued to offer misleading smiles, that in their complete insincerity gave morsels of false hope that led to nothing but more animosity.

If my years of teaching had been a sonata, I was at that time somewhere in the third movement, in which there were interludes of serving on textbook and curriculum committees, and helping to prepare for North Central Association's team, which would be evaluating us as a public school for state and national accreditation. I was still the sponsor of Chess Club, and Foreign Language Club. Most of the remainder of my time was spent grading papers, planning lessons for five different classes daily, and attending faculty and PTA meetings. School wasn't just a part of my life. It was my life.

That enormous building, housing eighty faculty members and almost twenty-four hundred students in its endless corridors, countless rooms, huge parking lots, and playing fields, needed special and loving care. The staff of custodians were friendly, patient, and dedicated people, who in many ways held the property together through the day and night shifts, and like all custodians I remembered from my own high school alma mater, Jan, Bill, Henry, Florence, Jacquie, Frank, Allen, Patrick, and Betty all performed their duties without complaint, mopping up bodily fluids, cleaning bubble gum off desks and toilet seats, sweeping up carelessly tossed paper wads, washing blackboards and windows, and scraping food off cafeteria walls, all through their stoic smiles, and uncomplaining manner.

I always hoped that my students would see and appreciate the awesome dignity that our school custodians showed daily, and that those kids would learn that real dignity showed itself most truly, not in people who rode in limousines, wore expensive designer clothes, or lived in sprawling mansions when not on their yachts, but rather in the sometimes lowly tasks and duties of daily life, when we are all most vulnerable to our composure slipping away from us. I wanted our students to know that real dignity could never be purchased, but rather it had to come of its own accord in our doing the right thing with willing and brave resolve, something that began in the heart and became genuine through the spirit. It was always good to know that the presence of all our custodians and cafeteria staff at school offered more good role models everyday than anyone could hope for.

Our office staff of Kelly, Joyce, and Margaret, were the people in charge of everything except setting broken bones and stopping severe bleeding. Those amazing ladies were the go-betweens of every crisis in the building. They were the ones through whom so much communication was done, and Joyce, the the head secretary, was really the one, not the principal, at the helm of the ship. From her many years of experience, she handled every problem like a master diplomat, defusing possible explosions from disgruntled parents, keeping track of all special program dates and where they would occur, and knowing where funds went in working with Margaret, the bookkeeper. Anyone who needed to know what had happened, what was happening, or what was going to happen in that little universe, known as

Morton High School, went to Joyce, our true oracle. Yet, through all the demands made upon her hourly, Joyce remained the picture of equanimity, the calm we needed for every storm, and the kind soul none of us really deserved.

If the hub of that miniature solar system was the main office, one of its satellites was certainly the teachers' lounge, a little world filled with blue smoke, vinyl-covered chairs, tables strewn with coffee cups and newspapers, and cratered areas, pock-marked by ashtrays of cigarette and cigar butts. There occasionally flared up little legends by students, who claimed they had experienced glimpses of that nether world through the blue haze that flowed into the hallway, whenever the door was opened. Even we teachers who didn't smoke managed to smell of tobacco after just a few minutes in that room. Today we talk of second-hand smoke, but in those days, being within the walls of the teachers' lounge was like being inside a hookah pipe or a smoke house.

I remember only one time that a student ever dared to walk into the teachers' lounge. She was an underclassman, carrying a message for Mrs. Kavin, who at the moment was taking her time over a well-deserved cup of java. Mr. Clifford Potts jumped up immediately, running toward the poor girl, while spouting words of rage and terror as though the Holy Grail had been found and defiled by some unspeakable sacrilege. Afraid that Clifford might actually strike the bewildered child, I ran to intercede, escorting her out the door and taking her note to Mrs. Kavin, who was still in a state of shock over the whole incident. Mr. Potts just fell into a chair, his face beet-red, as he wiped his forehead with a handkerchief before looking at me, as though he had just narrowly escaped a Bengal Tiger or the IRS. That entire episode taught me in a painful way how sacred that space was to some, and that infidels, otherwise known as students, were forbidden upon pain of death from entering, at least by some in the teacher hierarchy, who saw that room as a more hallowed place than the Pope's private apartments in the Vatican.

The teachers' lounge was also a place where gossip flourished, like seeds dropped into the best loam. Some of the talk was about other teachers, ones who were usually not there to defend whatever parts of their honor needed defense, rumors generally based upon tidbits as serious as alleged affairs, or as trivial as someone having worn clashing colors. Jane Austen would have loved all the delicious tittle-tattle condensed into that tiny fragment of the human situation with all its conflicts, rivalries, slander, and vanity, arranged so elegantly, as if on mahogany bookshelves.

The rest of the talk was usually about students, who had been caught cheating, whose parents were on the war path, or ready to be certified as mental cases, who was getting married or divorced, who had a new car in the parking lot, why the principal was a raving maniac, why eating the cafeteria corn dogs on a stick was probably not the best thing we could do for our health, and who would be retiring at the end of the school year. It was indeed a separate world from the one where people bought groceries, played pinochle, attended weddings, paid taxes, and watched toilet paper commercials on television. However, even a nursing home is its own little universe with its share of conflicts, celebrations, and rivalries. Wherever human beings are grouped together in a confined space everyday, whether in an office building or a nursery, human foibles will emerge daily and create a fabric of behavior that often makes people look less civilized than goldfish or antelope.

I don't know if Mr. Kelton, our principal, grew weary of chasing his toupee around the parking lot on windy mornings, or if our football team just wasn't winning enough games to suit him, but in 1989 he retired, moving to Florida with his wife Beverly to become a PR guru for a company that made men's hair products. The "gerbil" had a job.

Before I even met the new principal, I was impressed by her credentials. She had taught very successfully both Spanish and girls' physical education, coaching softball and tennis. Anyone who could balance two fields of endeavor, that were so many light years apart, had my vote. Her name was Miss Frances Denton, and when she spoke to the faculty for the first time, I was surprised that so much intelligence, sensitivity, and spirit could be housed by such a petite frame. Her voice was surprisingly sure of itself, but there was an authentic and sympathetic cadence in its tone. She called us, "you guys," but with a true ring of affection and respect that made it work without the slightest chime of insincerity or derision. Yes, she loved sports, but she had also taught and loved foreign language and had a tremendous regard for academics and the pursuit of intellectual quality. The custodial and office staffs, counselors, and cafeteria folks had already met with Miss Denton and were singing her praises even before that faculty meeting. I was going to like this woman.

Chapter 27 A Different Tune

At that faculty meeting during which we had been introduced to our new principal, Miss Denton, I glanced back several times at Miss Belle, who was sitting two rows behind me. It was apparent from her smiling and nodding in agreement with much of what Miss Denton was saying, that Miss Belle liked the new principal too. From that moment on, I thought of Miss Denton as an ally, who might be able to pull together the varied and opposing factions of our faculty by helping us all achieve a sense of common purpose and hope.

Our collection of student writing and art work called, BENDING DIAMONDS, won an award of high commendation from the National Council of Teachers of English. The letter and certificate came from our having submitted our book the previous summer, but judging always took months, due to submissions being sent to the NCTE from all over the United States. I immediately made photo copies of the award to send to the senior editors, who had graduated, many of whom were then college freshmen. I also gave the story to the school newspaper and phoned the HAMMOND TIMES to get the news into its next issue.

The letter had already been sent to our principal, who came to my classroom during my conference period to tell me how proud she was of the honor conferred upon our school for student writing. She said what a wonderful way it was for her to begin her duties as administrator, and that though she had nothing really to do with this academic award, she felt proud anyway to be entering a place that she was sure would continue to be honored for its academic work. Then taking my hand, she added that I could always depend upon her support for endeavors like BENDING DIAMONDS, which would help to make our students shine. In all my remaining years as sponsor of the school's literary anthologies, Miss Denton proved to be as good as her word. She always found money for the printing costs of the publications, so that I never again had to have another car wash, bake sale or beg-a-thon to raise funds. Being appreciated was a new feeling for me, one I had to get used to.

Of course, one of my other initial thoughts upon opening that letter of congratulations from the NCTE was to run directly to Miss Belle's room with a framed copy to hang over her desk. All the aspersions she had been casting on my attempts to inspire students to write well, especially in my Creative Writing class had, on one level, wounded me, and on another level had only increased my determination to protect and honor our students' best efforts at all kinds of writing. That thought bolstered my sense of purpose in the matter, but what happened next came as a new contingency that knocked some of the wind out of my sails.

Still feeling a bit high for the next few days after receiving news of the award and then Miss Denton's congratulatory visit, I learned that Miss Belle was starting what she called, "The Poetry Club." A brief article in the school newspaper explained that it would be a group meeting once a week, "for the purpose of studying in depth the great English and American poets." In a way, I was delighted and impressed by Miss Belle's evident dedication to poetry. On the other hand, there was no mention of the chance for students to create and discuss their own work. I knew that any extracurricular activity called, "Poetry Club" would probably fend off any boys, who would think the whole thing sounded just like another assignment, or some kind of "lovey-dovey stuff."

After a couple of weeks, I walked by Miss Belle's classroom on a Tuesday afternoon when her poetry club was supposed to be meeting. Glancing through the open door, I saw Miss Belle sitting at her desk, only two girls in student desks facing hers. The room was otherwise empty of people, but there was a record playing of a reading by Dylan Thomas of his poem, "Do Not Go Gentle Into That Good Night." The deep, rich, resonant quality of his voice drew me into the room, where I sat in the back row to hear the fire of his words.

"Do not go gentle into that good night,
Old age should burn and rave at close of day;
Rage, rage against the dying of the light."

I smiled at Miss Belle, who nodded her approval at my visit, as I listened to the sensuous, rhapsodic plea of Thomas for his father to fight against death, the poet's voice as rich and golden as fine old Cognac. The end of the meeting had evidently come with the conclusion of the recording, and Miss Belle dismissed the two girls, who smiled sweetly when they passed me as they left the room.

There were tears in Katherine Belle's eyes, but I couldn't tell if they were from the profound beauty of the Dylan Thomas reading of his dark poem on death, or that Katherine had seen the irony of using such a poem to end the meeting of a club that looked as though it too was probably facing its own demise. Taking a deep breath and trying to smile again, she looked at me to say, "Congratulations, John, on the award for the book of your students' writing. You must be very proud."

"Yes," I said. "I must admit feeling pride and satisfaction for the work our students did, and for the recognition they deserve."

"Don't be so modest, John. You merit recognition too for all your work with the kids on their writing," she continued.

"Thanks, Katherine. I appreciate your appreciation," I smiled.

She took out a handkerchief for her eyes as I was leaving the room. I looked back when reaching the door, and she appeared so small and frail among all those empty student desks, desks that would not see any more students in attendance at "Poetry Club." After I closed the door, I felt a wave of compassion for Miss Belle, that I had not experienced before, a woman I knew, who was deeply unhappy and someone at whom I could never be angry again, despite her stiff manner, one which I then knew was only a curtain behind which hid very deep emotion, sensitivity, and pain.

In the parking lot I ran into Jack Farrel, to whom I hadn't spoken since the day I had absconded with his WALL STREET JOURNAL from the teachers' lounge. He had always made me feel like an old wooden gate blown off its hinges in a high wind, so he was someone I made a conscious effort to avoid, whenever possible, but I had learned that he was in some ways like Miss Belle. They were both people who were unhappy themselves, unfulfilled but angry at the mere suspicion that there might be others who felt some measure of joy or even satisfaction in their lives. My experiences with both people would lead me to the unalterable conclusion that their stories were common, and that there were actually a great many other people whose lives were poisoned by the desire to make sure others were as miserable as they.

Jack leaned on the roof of his car, parked next to mine and peered over his sunglasses at me to say, “So, what’s this award thing I heard about?”

When I explained that our students were being honored for their creative writing and editing of an anthology of their own work, Jack’s right arm went up, his elbow still on the car roof and his head resting in his right hand, a look of astonishment on his face as he asked, “Are your sure those were OUR students?”

“Yes, Jack. Believe it or not, they were our students.”

“How do you get them to write?” he inquired.

“Sometimes they need motivation that goes beyond mere homework assignments,” I continued. “Then they begin to take pride in something they know is difficult but possible, and they start to meet the challenges of writing for writing’s sake. There’s more than one way to score a touchdown or a home run,” I said.

“Amazing, “ he responded. “Truly amazing. Well, I’m sure credit is due to you as well for inspiring them to write. I’ve heard good things from the kids about your writing classes. Congrats!” he concluded.

“Thanks, Jack,” I answered. “I hope only that we can live up to the standard the kids have set for themselves over the past year.”

After adjusting his sunglasses, Jack then got into his car and drove from the parking lot, where I sat in my own car for at least another five minutes before starting it, as I pondered what Jack Farrel had just said to me. It was like having received a sincere compliment from Don Rickles. I felt a bit stupefied and delighted at the same time, almost as though after many months, I had escaped from prison by slowly tunneling my way out with only a teaspoon in order to see light, blue sky and to smell the freshness of sea air at last. Adding this experience to the one with Miss Belle earlier the same afternoon, receiving her good wishes as well, was almost too much to accept as real. I was intoxicated by a feeling of happiness that probably comes far too seldom to any of us.

Chapter 28 Absence

It was October 20th, one of those cool, crisp evenings that smelled of woodsmoke and burning leaves, when pumpkins were on front porches, ready to become jack-o-lanterns in another few days. I had taken a walk, and after grading papers, watched on PBS the next installment of a series called ELIZABETH R, starring Glenda Jackson, about the life of Queen Elizabeth I of England. Going to bed at my regular time of ten o'clock, I had turned off the telephone but was awakened some time after midnight by the brass knocker on the front door. Through the peephole I was surprised to see a policeman. When I opened the door, he told me that my mother had been trying to phone me and that I should contact her right away, but he wouldn't tell me why.

My first attempt to call Mom yielded only a busy signal, but I reached her around 12:45 to hear her weary voice tell me that my father had passed away in his sleep just before midnight and that I should come as soon as possible.

My drive there seemed one of the longest of my life, and by that hour, there was a drizzle of rain that splashed sad messages on my windshield all the way. The porch light was on when I arrived at my parents' house on the other side of town, and my brother David's blue Chevrolet was parked in front. I didn't ring the bell but walked in to see my mother sitting on a sofa in the living room, sobbing, my brother sitting next to her with his arm around her. Mom wasn't wearing her glasses, but she was wiping her eyes with a handkerchief. She stood to give me a long hug, saying nothing yet as my brother then gave me a hug too.

"Shall I brew a pot of tea?" Mom asked.

"Yes, please," I answered, a little surprised at hearing those everyday words as the first ones spoken at a time when we were all three on the verge of going into some kind of shock, but maybe they were actually just the right words, ones that could postpone for a few moments the terrible reality of loss we would be facing together full-force, soon enough.

My dad had suffered a massive heart attack in his sleep and had only one convulsive movement, alerting my mother, who was still awake, reading in bed next to him. Calling 911, Mom felt no pulse and detected no breathing from Dad as she waited for the paramedics, who pronounced him dead just after midnight. The county coroner would be there soon.

I was remembering the last conversation Dad and I had only a week before when, in my parents' garden, I told him to mind his doctor in avoiding salt, alcohol, and cholesterol-laden foods of which Dad was so very fond. While flicking his extinguished cigarette away, Dad said simply, "Aw, doctors. Phooey!" Then he smiled at me in his impish way, as though his dismissive attitude might reduce the seriousness of my request.

My mother had fought a long and difficult battle with Dad about his taking prescribed medications and eating the right foods, while avoiding the bad ones. Mom's becoming a food Nazi was only partly effective in the sense that she couldn't monitor every simple move and decision made by her often obstinate husband, who, when my mother went through the swinging door to the kitchen, would take from his lapel or pocket one of the salt packets he had collected from the fast food places he was forbidden to visit, but which all knew him by name. Then he would put his forefinger to his lips in order to let the rest of us know that we shouldn't tattle on him to our mother, the warden.

Dad also kept a stash of giant milk chocolate bars, the kinds that could be used as building materials instead of bricks. His study was lined with bookshelves and books, the perfect hiding place for those big candy bars, salt packets, and bottles of brandy, none of which were found until after his death. His argument, however, had always been in favor of "quality of life over mere duration." He meant to have it his way, in defiance of any powers that be, which meant Mom and his heart doctor.

David and I entered the bedroom together to see our father lying on his back in the same position in which he had died. His face looked surprisingly restful, as though he were just sleeping. There was no hint of struggle or pain, only a relaxed remembrance of our dad that we would carry with us forever, a down comforter up to his chin, his silver hair shining in the light of the lamp next to the bed, the large pillow cradling his dear head.

My brother broke down in my arms, sobbing uncontrollably, so that I led him to a chair. His words were garbled, but I recognized the simple question, "Why?" which he repeated again and again, as though the force of asking it over and over would somehow bring an answer.

He and Dad had been best friends as far back as I could remember, playing their guitars together, going to baseball games and on fishing trips together, and sharing confidences that would be shared with no one else, not even Mom. There was something symbiotic in their similarity and loving partnership as father and son. They were cut from the same cloth, and their relationship was one I had always admired and envied at the same time. Though my mother, sister, and I were loved by Dad and David, my father and brother almost shared the same heart-beat and a psychic bond that transcended anyone's understanding, including their own. I knew that Dad's death was going to be even more horrible for David than for the rest of us. It was as though my brother's vital energy, his own life force, were going to be buried with Dad. The final blow that early morning came when the coroner and his team came and unceremoniously placed our father into a black plastic, zippered sack before carrying him out the front door. David collapsed from the sight, which he likened to our father having been removed in a trash bag. He wept for another forty minutes until there were no tears left, and he fell asleep on the sofa.

The wake at Bocken Funeral Home in Hammond was a continuous crowd, changing from minute to minute from the lines of people all the way down the block, a testimony to how respected and loved Dad was. Mom wore a black dress she had borrowed from one of her sisters, and sunglasses, even though we were indoors, because her eyes were so red from crying. Dad's funeral was even more packed than the wake had been, with wonderful tributes through speeches given by his friends and co-workers. His favorite guitar, an old Martin, was leaning against the casket, and I think that was what touched me more deeply than anything else that morning. I had such powerful and happy memories of Dad sitting alone in his study, playing his guitar with such skill and tenderness all the time I was growing up. That was my dad when he was most joyful and at his best.

The burial was difficult emotionally too, as are most other burials due to that terrible sense of finality, which some may call "closure," when the coffin is lowered into the grave, even if the sun is shining, as it was that day in an azure sky. The head of everyone there was bowed in prayer or at least in respectful silence, but I looked up at the life-size statues of Matthew, Mark, Luke, and John in a semi-circle, where Dad's grave was in the "Garden of the Apostles" at Chapel Lawn in Schererville, Indiana. The granite stone would be for Mom too, her name already carved there with only her date of birth. As the casket was lowered to the point of disappearing, I smiled at remembering that before the funeral at my parents' church, my sister Connie had slipped a giant milk chocolate bar into Dad's open casket, a gesture our dad would have appreciated and applauded.

There was a luncheon at the church after the burial with beautiful food prepared by the ladies of the congregation. Crowds of personal and family friends were there to comfort and energize our spirits as best they could, but for a few minutes my brother, sister and I slipped away to ponder some issues facing us. We half-jokingly decided that because Dad had been only one month from his retirement, the timing was certainly poor on one hand, that he wouldn't be able to enjoy the leisure he so deserved. On the other hand, the timing might have been a blessing in disguise, considering the fact that he and Mom would have been thrown together with no real release valve for Dad to escape Mom's incessant requests to fix screen doors, empty garbage, lift his feet every few minutes so she could vacuum underneath his chair, go to the store for milk or eggs, or wash a second-story window on which she had spied a smudge. No, in those terms, we decided that Dad's exit was perhaps better timed than anyone could really understand. We kidded one another that had he lived, there would probably have been a homicide within six months anyway with Dad as the prime subject of the evening news, and Mom's having achieved the true martyrdom she had always dreamed of.

Though I offered to keep Mom with me in the house I had purchased three years before, she decided to go with my sister to Nashville, Tennessee instead, where my sister had been living and working since 1984. Selling her house and most of its contents very soon after Dad's passing was a sign of Mom's wisdom in deciding not to allow any emotional festering to anchor her forever among mementos of the past, those material reminders of what she and Dad had shared since 1944. Putting her sentiments on hold, Mom started her new life in Tennessee, where she immediately made friends through the church that she and my sister attended. Aside from boxes of family photos, her sweet dog (a terrier named Benji), and items of jewelry Dad had bought for her, Mom let go of most of what could have so easily prevented her retreat into a new life. Taking a deep breath, she moved on with very little looking back.

One week after Dad's funeral, our brother David was in St. Margaret's Hospital with what his doctor told us were "sympathetic heart palpitations," resulting from our father's death and David's profound need to keep some kind of powerful connection, irrational as that might have been. That emotional tie between them was so strong, that in a strange way, my brother wasn't just grieving the loss of our father. He became our father.

I was happy to get back to school, even to the annoyances and problems of my work there, that would help to take my mind away from the pain of grief, which never goes away completely but subsides over time. School provided reasons to get up early each morning, giving me a sense of purpose through daily goals and projects with a hundred and fifty teenagers, who were somehow keeping me young.

Chapter 29 Coming Home Again

Life has a way of keeping us on its roller coaster of turns and sharp dips, so that as soon as we become complacent or comfortable, we can hit one of those steep slopes and have the wind knocked out of us again. At the same time, things level off, especially after difficult or tragic events, so that even being occupied by our work can bring about healing. After a death in the family, even the irritations of our jobs can help to take our minds away from the otherwise endless suffering that comes from that ultimate sense of loss. Though I don't want to devalue the significance of my work in teaching, it did serve as an important and welcome distraction for me after Dad's death.

When I got back to school, it was the final week of October and time for another homecoming, those five days of activities no one in his right mind would plan or even agree to at any other time of year without serious danger of being committed to one of those places, where he would be making pot holders out of pop-cicle sticks in a sunny day room somewhere. That year it was our team of varsity cheerleaders, who came up with the homecoming theme, which was CARNIVAL DAZE. My joy at being back at work brought me to more than one moment of weakness, when the cheerleaders were making the rounds for faculty volunteers to help with homecoming "festivities." Their cheerful enthusiasm was impossible to resist, and as soon as I agreed to participate in two of the events, I began to regret my having consented. One event would take place during the pep session seventh period on game day, Friday, and the other during the pre-game show that evening.

Foolishly perhaps, I agreed first to be a contestant in the "Hairiest Legs Competition" for male faculty, twelve of whom had volunteered to participate during the Friday afternoon pep session. We were all asked to wear cheerleader-type outfits and wigs, and to "ham it up" at the assembly, which we did, to the utter delight of the crowd. There was thunderous applause as we paraded coquettishly along the foot of the bleachers on both sides of the gym before stopping individually to allow the applause meter to measure the enthusiasm of our two thousand screaming fans. Relieved that I had not won the contest, I and the other losers filed out of the gym as the American Government teacher, Mr. Clinton, accepted his fur-covered trophy, pulling up his skirt one more time to show off one of the hirsute legs that had won the coveted statuette. I congratulated myself at having my dignity shredded for a good cause, when I knew that men like the Marx Brothers had done similar things for huge money in Hollywood. For years afterward, whenever I ran into former students from that era, they always alluded to that hairy legs contest in some detail, and I began to wonder about the possibility of combining hairy legs contests with academic material, like irregular French verbs, or English grammar, which if successful, would change our entire educational system forever, in helping students remember everything they were taught by mere association through laughter.

The worse of the two events was the pie-throwing extravaganza, which was based upon customers paying three dollars to throw a "cream pie" at a member of the school faculty. The pie was actually a heavy paper plate, weighted by half a plum and covered with shaving cream. There were fourteen of us on the faculty, who agreed to be part of this dignity-shrinking event, each of us wearing a plastic poncho and shower cap for the ordeal of being pelted by a pie. Miss Belle, Mr. Potts, and Mr. Farrel refused to partake in the "fun," which was a real shame financially, because had they been targets for those pies, the school could have raked in enough money to build a new wing of classes and another swimming pool. As it was, only two students chose me as their target, one girl, who missed hitting me altogether, and a boy, whom I had given an "F" for a recent book report on a volume called CYCLE SLUTS. He managed a direct hit, so that for the next couple of days, I smelled like Old Spice with a hint of plum, but I was happy to have done my part, for the first time in my life, in supporting a series of events centered around a football game, something that as a rule wasn't even on my list of things that mattered.

We won the homecoming game against Clark High School, and the following Monday as after every other homecoming week, we got back to whatever might have been called "normal." It was already November with Thanksgiving, Christmas, and the new year on their way during those winter months that included the beginning of second semester, time flying by almost as fast as it seemed to during summer vacations.

Not every pupil I had in my classes over the years was a success story for me. Like other teachers, I usually saw any student's failure as at least partly my own. When my bag of tricks was empty, and the student was still acting like public enemy number one, and/or in danger of not getting a credit, especially for a required course, I couldn't help but take it, on some level, personally.

Bradley Foster was a freshman in one of my English classes, but he was not a student I could include in any list of my teaching successes. While he was in my class, I felt continually defeated by variables upon which I seemed to have no effect. His being in my English class was, for me, like waiting for the mail to come with a big check, but after weeks of no delivery, realizing the check wasn't going to arrive, no matter what my efforts were to make it happen.

Brad had come from an inner city Chicago school, where the process of expulsion had already begun when his parents moved to Indiana, and most of us on the faculty suspected that this was the reason they were moving in the first place. My only consolation was that reports from some of his other teachers were even more horrific than mine. The faculty code name for Brad was, "Dillinger," not because he carried a gun or robbed banks, but because he seemed completely amoral.

The day he was brought to my classroom by his counselor, Mrs. Davis, was when I knew we were all in for some unusual experiences with this kid. The nervous look in Mrs. Davis's shifting eyes was my first clue that something was amiss, because she always seemed to have a good handle on every situation. I had never seen anything or anyone rattle her, so if that Rock of Gibraltar appeared to be uneasy, I wondered what might be around the next corner.

Brad was a boney-looking kid with limbs that seemed too long for his torso. He was all elbows and knees. His dark brown hair was of medium length, cut straight across in bangs over eyebrows of the same shade, eyebrows that appeared to join over his nose, like a single, unyielding, dark line above his green eyes. His lips looked hard, as if moving them into anything like a smile might break them. He had the face of someone whose motto in life might easily have been, "Me against the world." I couldn't tell at first if his menacing appearance was deliberately used as a shield against being hurt, or if it was simply the way his face was built.

As I always did for other new students, I took him to the front of the class to introduce him quickly before giving him an unobtrusive desk, where he would not have to feel examined by the rest of the class. Then I gave him a class enrollment card to fill out along with a grammar book and literature text. He didn't have a pen, so I lent him a blue ball point with my initials on it in gold before returning to the front of the room to continue our lesson on the short story, "Harrison Bergeron" by Indiana author, Kurt Vonnegut, Jr. It was a narrative with which I was enjoying a sense of progress and genuine interest among my freshmen. In our discussion about the strange, future world of Vonnegut's story, we dwelt upon the relatively new expression, "political correctness" and what it might mean in our year of 1990, even though the story was from the early 1960's. The questions and comments that morning were fast and furious, which made me happy that Brad could begin by seeing that other students were intrigued enough to be engaged in their own commentary.

My eye went back to Brad occasionally to see if he was registering any kind of reaction to what the class was doing, but he manged to continue looking like an exhibit in a wax museum. In that way, he reminded me of Danny Pinkerton from a few years before. I couldn't tell if his zombie-like behavior was from shyness, obstinacy, or just complete indifference.

When the bell rang at the end of class, there were two students at my desk with questions about the homework, so my plan for assigning buddies to help Brad would have to wait. After the room was empty of students, I noticed that Brad's books were still on his desk, along with the enrollment card I had asked him to fill out with the pen I had lent him. The card was still blank, but my pen was gone. This was not a good beginning, but I was resolved to keep trying to find out, if I could, what made Brad tick. According to the records from his previous school, the only class for which he had the chance of receiving a credit was wood shop, and even that was only a "D." Storming this castle wasn't going to be easy. There were alligators in the moat.

For the next three days, Brad left his books on his desk and brought no paper with him to class, so I politely refused to give him another pen. When he slouched down in his seat, I made him sit up straight. The battle of wills had begun, and I knew that it was time to enlist the help of one or both of his parents to get Brad on a path to some kind of success in school, which as a teacher, I still believed could be a springboard to success in the "outside" world.

The incident that finally made me contact Brad's mother came at the end of class, when I caught up with Brad at the door to hand him his literature book for reading the next story, which was Ray Bradbury's "The Sound of Thunder." Brad gave me only a brief and expressionless gaze before dropping the book at my feet and saying, "I don't feel like it, man. I never done no homework before, and I ain't gonna start now." Then he turned and walked away, as though he had just told me to have a nice day. Thoughts of reporting his insubordination ran through my head in that moment, but I knew that such measures had undoubtedly been tried before without effect, so I had to come up with something else for the time being. His reaction had floored me, as I suppose it had been meant to do, but I went immediately to the nearest phone in the English office, called downstairs for Brad's phone number, and then called his house.

A woman answered, and in a raspy, barroom voice that reminded me of Thelma Ritter or Selma Diamond, She said, "Yeah, what d'ya want?"

"Hello, is this Mrs. Foster?" I asked

"Sure. What of it?" she replied.

"Mrs. Foster, this is John Bolinger from Morton High School, and I'm Brad's English teacher. Do you have five minutes or so to talk with me about your son?"

"Oh, brother, this oughta be good. Go ahead, JB. Shoot," she continued.

"I want to help your son earn the credit he needs for my class toward graduation, and I was hoping that you, his mother, who knows him best, could give me some advice."

"Hey, I don't know what to tell ya, Mr. Bolinger. Brad has always been the way he is right now. His dad and I haven't been able to change him, but I sure wish ya luck. Let me know how things turn out."

With that, she simply hung up on me, and I knew that whatever battle was on its way, I'd have to face it alone. Brad's other teachers had given up on him, and I was beginning to see that using all my energy to try helping a kid, who didn't care at all, might be a complete waste of time for us both. At every turn so far, he had spurned any assistance. Even his counselor had all but given up, except to recommend that Brad be sent to the Career Center on the other side of town, where he could take classes in automotive mechanics, carpentry, or electricity. This, in fact, was the solution that even Brad and his parents agreed to at last.

On the day Brad was taken by bus to the Career Center for the first time, I found on my desk a copy of the homecoming issue of our school newspaper, THE MORTONITE. The front page was face-up, and the photo of participants in the "Hairiest Legs" competition had a big question mark in ink next to a circle around me in the picture. The pen laid on top of the paper was the initialed blue one I had lent to Brad weeks before. I never saw or heard from him again, but I always imagined that he would be all right and on his way to becoming an auto mechanic, carpenter, or electrician.

Chapter 30 Blame It on Count Chocula

By the 1990's, whining had become one of America's chief pastimes. Even while grocery shopping, I was unceasingly annoyed by the more and more familiar sound of childish whimpering in places like the cereal aisle, where a kid would moan demands, like "Awww, Mommy, I want this cereal, pleeease!"

"No," would come the first response. "Chocolate Rasberry Sugar Bombs are not good for you."

"Awwww, that's not fair, Mommy!" was often the comeback, which would usually only prolong the debate until the mother would at last give in by saying, "Oh, all right, but only for small portions. I don't want to pay for any dental implants until you're at least twelve."

These collective grocery store experiences became, over time, the basis of my theory that many of our social ills can be traced back to the cereal aisles of grocery stores across the country, among all those hundreds of brands of tooth-rotting breakfast fare, with colorful and humorous logos on the boxes, reinforced on Saturday morning television commercials, mesmerizing children into believing that all that sugar was as vital as the air they breathed.

Finally, it was almost as though these children from all across America had banded together at secret meeting sites, when their parents thought their kids were really playing on monkey bars, riding their bikes, or skate boarding. This facade covered the fact that the kids were actually meeting to share their new national message of, "WHINING WORKS!" Playgrounds everywhere became convention centers to spread the word that, not only could grocery store griping and sniveling bring results, but such intense complaining could also bring rewards in other sectors of society. Thus, whining made its way into public schools, where its effect on scholastic standards may still be seen in the demands placed upon classes of our public schools, which I believe sometime during the past twenty years managed to merge with the entertainment industry.

Another result of this huge bellyaching business has been that certain teachers across the land have banded together in a counter-movement, the crux of which is that homework requirements should remain stringent, and that all teachers for all grades in public schools must join together in building a mass immunity to the lamentations of those students, who have honed complaining down to an art form, which has seeped into factories, courthouses, the auto and garment industries, food production, and to every other conveyor belt, literal and figurative, that produces shoddiness as its chief product, rather than standing up to the laziness of moaning shirkers of duty in living up to higher, albeit more difficult, expectation.

The more I encountered the tired old phrase from my students of "That's not fair," the more I became resolved to live up to a teacher headline I longed to see on the front pages of newspapers across the country, TEACHERS FIGHT BACK WITH MASS WHINING OF THEIR OWN! Of course, that story never actually hit the news stands, but its significance became my focus in the attempt to help squelch the national whining fest, that had already been going on for years.

I began practicing an irritatingly nasal tone of voice in my use of important whining terminology as in, “Awww, you guys can read all twenty pages in one night. Breaking them up into little baby assignments would just be silly, and that’s not fair!” If students persisted, I would plug my ears with my forefingers and walk around the classroom singing, “Alouette.” After a while, perhaps to avoid the torture of my increasingly professional whining skills, they stopped arguing and just did the assignments. This technique was far more successful than my earlier one, which was doubling an assignment (with an attempted straight face) and then cutting it in half to make it seem they were getting away with something. That method was not only devious, but my acting was never quite good enough to pull it off, because apparently, despite my best efforts, there always remained the hint of a smirk on my face and just enough inauthenticity in my voice, that even the slowest kid in the class was on to me.

So, the next time you want to know what’s wrong with America, in terms of our shrinking standards of quality, go to your nearest super market, get a shopping cart, and mosey on over to the cereal aisle, that wonderland of sugar-impregnated breakfast vittles with about as much nutritional value as bubblegum, and observe the children there and the interaction with their parents, the outcome of which will almost assuredly be a mother caving in to her child’s demand for a marshmallow cereal with soda pop overtones, in order to avoid the screeching, high-pitched and embarrassing hint of abuse that might carry over into the soup and condiments aisle. This, dear friends, is really the source of all irrational and unmerited sense of entitlement in our country, the only remedy to which may be a good dose of homework. If all else fails, then just blame everything on Count Chocula and that awful sugar rush our kids have come to require.

Chapter 31 Aunt Mae

Mae was the sister of my paternal grandfather, and when I was a child, my older cousin Richard's calling her "Great Aunt Mae" confused me into assuming that she was simply a terrific lady. The fact that she was my dad's aunt somehow escaped me. Every time she came to visit, she gave me a crisp new dollar bill, so it was easy for me to think of her as being pretty great. Genealogy, for me, had nothing to do with it. She was a very nice lady who gave me a buck whenever we met.

Aunt Mae had lived in Pennsylvania much of her life, raising two daughters, many of those years as a widow before she moved to Washington, D.C. and worked as a stenographer for the United States Senate. Though she was industrious and energetic, Aunt Mae responded to the shock of Uncle Henry's death in 1951 by never letting go of her sense of fashion from that year. Like so many other women, who have suffered the sudden and tragic losses of husbands, Aunt Mae seems to have put something permanently on pause, perhaps as a kind of anchor that kept her moored safely in that happier time before her husband died. For Mae, her clothing style froze in 1951, never changing at all until her own death in the 1990's. To accomplish this personal suspension of the otherwise unceasing movement and development of fashion, Aunt Mae had to have her clothes made to order, so that even through the 1980's and much of the 1990's she remained a fashion plate from 1951, untouched by time or the changes in women's wear all around her. The Dior-style suits, silk blouses, hats, and shoes, all in the style of 1951, made her stand out in any crowd, partly because she was so statuesque. She always wore her double strand of white pearls too, but it was her tortoise shell glasses that intrigued me most, adding to the very tailored and academic look that made her unique, if not completely eccentric.

Anyone who remains unaffected by clothing fashions for almost fifty years will also have strong opinions, impervious to the many swirls of change and disagreement all around. That was Aunt Mae, a woman of powerful conviction that often spilled into severe judgments on everything from how to brew tea to what the President should be doing (and she would write to let him know from time to time). Also a woman of kind heart, she always meant to be helpful and never thought of herself as interfering in any way, but rather through her healthy ego, she saw herself as the solution to almost any predicament.

Aunt Mae was eighty-seven years old when she wrote to me that she would be paying a visit. The last time I had seen her was when she stayed with Mom for a few days after Dad's death in order to help Mom get through at least the first part of that ordeal. Now that Mom was living with my sister in Tennessee, it would be my guest room that would accommodate dear Aunt Mae for her sojourn away from Washington. Knowing how fastidious she could be, I ironed every pillow case and napkin, and gathered up as many remaining molecules of dust I could find. Over the phone my mother wished me luck, and I could hear my sister Connie laughing in the background saying, "She'll have him standing in a corner after two days."

When I picked up Aunt Mae at O'Hare Air Port in Chicago that windy March afternoon, I was surprised to see that, even at age eighty-seven, she was still as majestic as I remembered from my childhood. She was wearing a tweed suit with black felt beret, like the ones she had worn since before Eisenhower was elected President. After retrieving her luggage, we stopped for tea at one of the air port shops, where Aunt Mae and I caught up on respective news items from the family out east and in Indiana, the sometimes tabloid doings of our remaining relatives, including those of my father's only remaining sibling, Uncle Jesse, who had retired from Inland Steel and started his own lawn mower repair business from his own home.

Aunt Mae expressed her disappointment regarding my brother David, whom she considered a "misguided hippie," only because she hadn't seen him since the early 1970's, when at a family reunion kind of picnic at Wicker Park, David had sported jeans, a psychedelic shirt, long hair, and a beard. It's true that among my very conservative cousins, my brother did stand out, considering that those cousins were the only people I knew who wore neckties to picnics, and I guess the family photo taken of all twenty-seven of us said it all. My brother looked like Jesus Christ on dope among a crowd of others, who appeared to be Baptist missionaries with their wives and children too perfect for me to believe hadn't been rented somewhere for the day. Aunt Mae took a copy of that photo from her purse as we sipped our tea. My assurances that David was a good citizen, fine husband, and terrific father were to no avail until later during Aunt Mae's visit, when I had my brother, his wife, Peggy, and their son Dave over for a dinner during which Aunt Mae's view of my brother softened as she became convinced what a wonderful man he was and how cogent he was in conversation. His not having a bong pipe with him helped too, of course.

Aunt Mae insisted upon visiting my classes at school, where she said she would be perfectly content to sit quietly in the back of the room to observe the "educational process" and compare it to the one she remembered from her own school days. Because I could never deny her anything, it was a done deal. She accompanied me to school for five days of her visit, during which she met the office staff, chatted happily with custodians, and during my conference period even wandered the halls, talking to random students in every locker bay, had lunch with the faculty, learning many of their names, and they hers.

When I introduced her to my Basic English II class, I heard a voice whisper, "Oh, my God! There really is a time machine!" The students were fascinated that my aunt was eighty-seven and that she was taking stairs without even a cane. Considering that most teenagers think thirty is pretty old and that at forty, people should probably be in wheel chairs, Aunt Mae's being eighty-seven absolutely bowled them over and made them quite respectful, even when she corrected their grammar. She was not pleased that some of the students called me, "Mr. B." My explanation that this was done out of a blend of respect and genuine affection did little to assuage her concern that the world was toppling into chaos.

On Friday afternoon she said goodbye to the office staff, who seemed to adore her. Then she walked up the stairs to exchange farewells with three or four other faculty members whose classes she had also observed during that week. As I watched her climb those stairs, I noticed her slowing down just a little toward the top, grasping the railing and wincing, as if in pain. It may have been that she was just sad to be leaving, but I saw her in that moment for the first time as an actual, elderly person, someone for whom all those years had accumulated through her sense of wonder, innocence, determination, and love of people and life itself.

The contrast between her in the old fashioned clothes, and the hard, unyielding stairs of that modern building made her appear to me like a hauntingly beautiful and ancient Gregorian Chant played on some rock radio station, but it was that unfeeling modern backdrop that seemed out of place, not Aunt Mae. As she disappeared down the hallway, I continued to stand at the foot of the stairs, overcome with a sense of pride in this woman, whose life had spread out like a finely patterned carpet over most the 20th Century, a life that had defied the groaning pessimism and fear of growing old by always reaching for the next adventure, the next level in that long corridor with so many doors, all of which she wanted to enter. Because of her, I would never again fear growing old, if I could only remember my fearless and loving Aunt Mae, who died in 1998 at the age of ninety-three. After her death, Deborah, Mae's only surviving daughter, mailed a package to my mother. It was a little jewelry case containing the double stand of pearls of which Aunt Mae had always been so proud.

Chapter 32 Curve Ball

When I was in high school, I never thought there might be battles waged between academics and sports. It just never occurred to me that strife could exist between a coach and an academic teacher over whether a student would be eligible to play in a game against another school. It all came down to the conflict between the integrity of an academic teacher's standards versus the school's public face in a sports event. It was almost impossible to make the two sides match up. One side or the other had to give in.

Jasper Stickley was a senior in my writing class that spring of 1994, a pleasant enough kid, but one who more often than not, failed to turn in assignments. My talks with him about the danger of his failing my class came to little, except the usual two-cent excuses and enough pledges of good faith that, had they been promissory notes, would have assured my retirement to some luxurious villa in Tuscany.

A tall, square-jawed red-head of inordinately good looks, Jasper was especially popular with the girls, and I mean not just the senior ladies, but juniors, sophomores, and even the lowly freshmen damsels, who swooned over him as though he were a rock star. It was said that girls from many classes would rush to whatever room Jasper was going to or leaving, and they would try to look nonchalant as they followed like a swirling cape behind him. Perfectly aware of his status, Jasper, I believe, enjoyed it all thoroughly, but in my class, he seemed easily distracted by the girls who sat all around him, like a devoted harem.

There were times when the mere turning of a head, the flipping of long hair, or the crossing of legs by the girls had Jasper's utter attention, and of course, he also had their attention in the sense that his sneeze or twirling of a pencil was far more engaging than my song and dance in front of the room could ever be. This mutual admiration society in that cluster of seats made my gig much more challenging so that at times, even if I had tap danced with great vigor on top of my desk, few in that little group would have noticed. It was, as in any other classroom, all about competition, to the extent that I had to enthrall them enough with each lesson to put sexual diversions on hold until the bell rang for class to be dismissed. Anyone who has taught teenagers in a class with both boys and girls will tell you that keeping everyone's attention for an hour is somewhat like trying to climb Mount Everest while wearing flip-flops instead of boots.

In any event, there we all were, Jasper's spinning pencil far more entrancing than any tricks I had up my sleeve, and Jasper weeks behind on paying me the I.O.U.'s of homework he had not been turning in. I had already mailed a deficiency notice to Mr. and Mrs. Stickley, who had promised me that Jasper would be submitting all his late assignments. The big problem was that report cards were only one week away, and our varsity baseball game with Hammond High, only two weeks away. As our team's star pitcher, Jasper was a key player in every game, but, because of school rules carved in stone, any failing grade on his report card would bar him from participating in any sports event.

All this brought a visitor to my classroom during my conference period three days before report cards came out. Coach Mallory was in a frenzy about Jasper's deficiency notices from my class and from the chemistry class. It seems that our baseball coach was on the verge of clinching a "deal" with Mr. Koch, Japser's chemistry teacher, who said he would give Jasper an incomplete, even though Jasper had not done his homework for several weeks in that class either and had failed most quizzes and exams. Having given Jasper too much time and entitlement already though, I was not prepared to indulge him any further in granting yet more time to fulfill assignments that everyone else had turned in. That is exactly what I told his parents and what I told Coach Mallory, who, after hearing that I was not going to honor Jasper's laziness, acted as though I had just created a massive billboard insulting, in the most vulgar ways, the Queen of England. Mallory's verbal response was simply, "Well, John, this puts a heavy responsibility on your shoulders."

"Oh?" I asked. "And all this time I thought it was Jasper's responsibility. You'd better have a talk with HIM. Or maybe, if this game is so important, you should work on having the school change the rule about athletes who are failing classes being disqualified from game participation."

Smiling, the coach left my classroom, quietly closing the door behind him. Perhaps naively, I actually believed that encounter to have been the end of the matter, the ball being then in Jasper's court. I waited and hoped during those final days before report cards for assignments to be turned in by our star pitcher, but nothing was given to me as those few remaining days sped by. My anxiety grew almost hourly, until the day before teachers were all supposed to turn in their grades to be scanned and mailed. Jasper was absent that Thursday.

When I phoned his mother, she told me that her son was, "under the weather" and would certainly be in school the next day. I reminded her about the rather large backlog of work he had not submitted, and that he would receive a failing grade, not the cavalry riding in to rescue him again with another "incomplete." Everything depended upon his turning in a substantial amount of work the next day, especially the original short story, even though the pressure on me to grade it the next morning before grades were due would be considerable, since I had other classes to teach. Mrs. Stickley assured me that her son would be submitting work the next morning. I thanked her but decided not to shoot off any bottle rockets just yet. I had learned over twenty-five years of teaching, that striking bargains for grades at the last minute with students, especially athletes, yielded very mixed results, too many oaths to turn in overdue work having been broken like potato chips under dropped bowling balls. I didn't want students to get used to being "in debt" and believing that it was normal to be so.

After school a delegation of girls from Jasper's fan club came into my room, surrounding my desk, Susan Smutko having evidently been elected spokesman to beg me to pass Jasper so that he could pitch in the game the following week. Waiting for my response, which didn't seem to come quickly enough, the seven girls tilted their heads and whined in choral unison, "Awww, Mr. B. This is soooo important."

"Have you told Jasper how important it is?" I asked. "You know this is all up to him. You can't dump it on me at this point. I want him to pass, but he has to be a participant. No one is going to gift-wrap a passing grade for somebody, who isn't even trying."

That was it. Nothing else was said, and the group left the room in the most dejected way, their shoulders slumped and heads down. The extreme melodrama of their exit almost made me laugh.

The next day was Friday, grades due by noon, and the big game one week away. I was at school early, seven o'clock, in fact, anxious to receive the written work Jasper had sworn he would be turning in. At seven-thirty he entered my classroom, holding a folder of typed assignments. I heaved a sigh of relief as he laid the folder on my desk, smiling proudly as he did it. I reminded him that the most important piece of work was the short story, and he told me it was there too. Things were looking up, and I could already hear the roar of the crowd on game night, cheering for Jasper as he pitched a no hitter game with no one wanting to assassinate me for having failed him for that grading period. Life was good, and it appeared that my life might even continue.

Of course, I wanted desperately for things to be simpler in this case than they actually were, and I'm embarrassed to admit that as a seasoned teacher, I should really have known better than to have made such a shamelessly optimistic leap of faith when I saw that folder with Jasper's name on it that morning. Wishful thinking, however, is sometimes the most effective eraser of tough realities, the kinds that make us believe that we're all-knowing, when actually we don't know squat.

In the twenty minutes remaining before first period, I began going through the papers, especially happy that Jasper had included the most important assignment for the grading period, the original short story, which had been the principal homework over the previous six weeks. His title page read, "Best Intentions" by Jasper Stickley. Typed neatly, the pages drew me in to begin reading what Jasper had composed. Impressed by the descriptive detail, the character development, the main conflict, and the often witty phrasing, I couldn't put down the manuscript until the bell rang, and my first period French class began filing into the room.

Even as I was going through oral drills of French irregular verbs and pronunciations of feminine versus masculine adjectives, my mind drifted back to Jasper's short story and the deep familiarity of its style and theme. Knowing that I had to turn in my grades by noon to the main office, I also knew that I had to deal with the growing apprehension that was getting clearer by the minute in my mind about that story. Something was wrong, and I had to find out quickly what it was. During my next class, French IV, students had a fifteen-minute written exercise to complete, which gave me time to go through a stack of folders in my filing cabinet for previous Creative Writing classes.

In a folder of student work from three years before, I found a short story by a senior named Jay Fredricks. His narrative was called, "Cross Purposes." Aside from Jasper's title of, "Best Intentions," the two stories were identical, right down to the few errors in spelling and punctuation. Jasper had simply photocopied Jay's entire story and merely given it a different title. My heart sank, as I remembered some other kids' plagiarisms, sometimes humorously obvious examples like, Debbie Brown's copying one of Elizabeth Barrett Browning's "Sonnets from the Portuguese," or another senior boy claiming to have written the famous poem, "We Real Cool" by Gwendolyn Brooks, the then Poet Laureate of Illinois, or yet another student submitting a poem he had stolen from an awful song by the rock group, Limp Biscuit. Jasper's theft, however, was the most upsetting to me of them all, mostly because I had given him my trust to do the right thing, and even had he turned in a third-rate narrative, it would have given him a passing grade, because it would actually have been his own work based upon my main purpose in the writing class of honoring individuality, originality, and finding one's own voice, whatever that turned out to be.

Writing a terse comment on the last page of the story Jasper had turned in, I also stapled another photocopy of Jay's original story with the original title. It didn't even seem necessary to write an "F" on the paper. Jasper would certainly be able to deduce my meaning. At eleven-thirty I turned in all my grade sheets, which included for the writing class, Jasper's "F" in effort, "C" for conduct, and "F" for scholarship. During the writing class that afternoon, I gave back Jasper's folder with written comments on all the papers, including two poems which had also been plagiarized, one from Gary Snyder, and the other from Elizabeth Bishop, both internationally known poets. After class, Jasper stood in front of my desk, looking at the floor as he asked if there was any chance for a passing grade or at least an incomplete.

"What do YOU think, Jasper?" I asked

"I don't know," he answered.

"Then it seems that you've learned exactly nothing, Jasper. You'll have to weather the rest of this storm yourself. You're the one who created it in the first place."

Saying nothing more, even though he continued standing there a full two minutes longer, Jasper finally left the room, as I clenched my head in my hands, very close to sobbing.

Report cards were mailed that afternoon, which meant they would reach every student's home by Tuesday, but word of Jasper's failing grade in my class would have reached all ears by Monday morning. I could already feel the storm brewing through a terrible rumble of discontent among all those in our school and community for whom the coming baseball game was more important than The Second Coming. Though I felt unrealistically secure in the evidence I had for Jasper's having tried to cheat his way into a passing grade, I still didn't fully grasp the highly emotional implications of my having done the "honorable" thing. I knew only that I would never be able to live with myself for rewarding someone for such a huge deception, which was really also a kind of theft. Even though I didn't want to be self-righteous about it, I was also aware that I had to do what I knew was the right thing, ultimately for Jasper's sake as well as for my own. The awful collision between doing the true and honest thing versus what was simply popular had become one of the most difficult tests of my life. Everything I had tried to teach my students about living in an authentic way and writing honestly was now on the line.

Tuesday morning the assistant principal, Mr. Poteja, appeared between classes in front of my desk. This rare appearance made me know immediately that he was there to persuade or cajole me into changing the grade of our star pitcher and to put me in the unenviable position of saving the day at the cost of my own conscience. That, in fact, was precisely the reasoning for his "impromptu" visit. His argument was that the grade I gave Jasper would affect the whole school and even the entire community.

Reminding Mr. Poteja that Jasper had always been the one in charge of his own grade, I also asked what message we would be sending Jasper if we gave him a fake and completely unmerited grade on a silver platter. I then added that I didn't think that even a very public baseball game was worth our throwing our academic standards, along with our integrity into the dumpster. After a decidedly indignant "Hrumph," Mr. Poteja made his exit before my next class came in.

During the next two days, three faculty members, including the churlish Clifford Potts, snubbed me openly, and in the halls, whispers were unabashedly directed with deliberately increased volume in my direction with names like, "Louse," "Creep," and even "Bastard." After school on Wednesday, I was distressed to find that my car had been egged, some of the broken shells still sticking to the roof and hood, and the egg carton on the ground behind the trunk.

The principal, Miss Denton, talked with me to let me know she was on my side and that standing my ground was important in the broader view, which down the road would vindicate me and support the values I was trying so hard to protect.

All of this was a turning point for me in teaching, partly because the conflict put everything I believed in some kind of relief and gave me a new perspective on why I was in the profession, what I was trying to convey as an educator, and how we could all help to make students better people by overcoming some of their foibles, as well as teachers overcoming their own. Of course, none of this rhetoric had any immediate effect on some for whom that baseball game, in all its laser-sharp immediacy, was the only thing that mattered.

I never found out who had egged my car, and the thought haunted me for weeks afterward that the same lovely girls, who had been cooing over my desk to rescue their beloved Jasper, could easily have been the culprits. Jasper's having been rendered ineligible by the grade he had failed to earn in my class and our losing that game to Hammond High didn't help either. For the rest of that semester I remained about as popular as a rattlesnake in a big rabbit hutch, but like the times I had established my views on good attendance by going to homes of truants, this Jasper episode had confirmed that I believed that honest work should trump popularity and certainly cheating. I still doubt that there were any students or faculty, who didn't know that, even the "eggers."

Chapter 33 Recognizing Your Calling

One annoyance that at the time can seem unbearable, but that later on can become a blessing, is having a job when you're young that you truly hate, even if just for a little while. That detested employment can make one appreciate his true calling even more when it comes along, and can inspire anyone to keep looking for that occupational niche that fits him or her best, simply by making him want to escape whatever job is dull, meaningless, laborious, or just tedious.

My very worst days in teaching were all far better than even my best days at Inland Steel in Gary, Indiana. The summer of 1968 I worked on the Cold Strip Number Three in Gary for a couple of months, but my time on that job would forever after make me grateful that it had not become my life's work. Being there even for that short time helped me to comprehend and esteem the profession of teaching high school.

My most representative recollection of that summer at Inland was the first day, when I was an obvious green horn, wearing my brand new stiff, heavy work boots, clothes, and hard hat. Add to those the bug-eyed goggles, and you've conjured up the picture of a deep-sea diver. Our foreman, Joe Flint, was a sadistic, beer-bellied brute, about forty years old, who seemed to enjoy making everyone around him as uncomfortable as he could. He loved showing off his authority in ways that would embarrass anyone over whom he thought he had power. The fact that he never uttered a sentence without a double negative and at least three curse words made him less colorful than just plain mean and hopelessly stupid. One of those people who enjoyed looking down on others, Flint was also an open racist and made himself feel superior at the expense of those round him. Their pain and humiliation seemed to lift his spirit (if he had one).

The first day, Flint announced that he needed the college students for a special job. Sam, Frank, and I stepped forward to be informed by the smirking Flint that we would be spending the day cleaning dead rats, and maybe a few live ones, out of the grease pits. I'll never forget the three of us up to our ankles in oil and grease, shoveling dead rats, Flint looking down on us from above, laughing as we three slipped around the pit, wiping our sweaty brows with our greasy gloves and sleeves.

It became increasingly clear over the summer how much Flint hated us, despite our humility and obedience. Perhaps all of his animosity was based upon the fact that he was keenly aware of our temporary presence there, and that we three would be moving on to other jobs, where we could find a sense of fulfillment and happiness that Flint had never found and probably never would. There was, according to Frank, a terrible jealousy in Flint's nature that always surfaced whenever any of us three college students, whom Flint called "college stooges" did something right, which admittedly wasn't all that often. Those times he would simply scoff at us, never encouraging us in any way that we were on the right track. When, however, we did something wrong, he would laugh gleefully, as when Sam slipped on a patch of grease and badly cut his left arm on the razor edges of a giant steel coil one morning and was rushed to the infirmary, where he had thirty-seven stitches. Afterward, Flint laughed himself breathless in repeating the story of the "dumb-ass college twerp" to anyone who would listen.

My contempt for Flint was always clear to me, but my pity for him didn't materialize until near the end of the summer, when I began to find that everyone else at the plant hated him too, even more than we three lowly students did. He was reviled by everyone else but continued to believe that his cruel and contemptible behavior was somehow humorous, entertaining, and admired. I found this rather sad, but at the end of the summer, Frank, Sam, and I joyfully left Inland Steel, none of us saying goodbye to Flint, who had never offered even one word of hope or kindness to any of us. As our bus pulled away from the plant, and Cold Strip #3 grew smaller behind us, I pictured Flint remaining a wretched and empty man into old age, vilified by all who knew him. That thought softened the disgust and loathing that I needed to leave behind.

Despite the awful experiences of that summer, I had learned at least one valuable lesson, that whatever authority I was to be given as a school teacher, I would never use it to scorn, embarrass, or hurt anyone. Flint would remain the standard for everything I abhorred about our weaknesses as a species. Whenever I felt myself becoming the least bit mean-spirited, cruel, overbearing, or arrogant, I would remember Joe Flint and be instantly horrified by the mere possibility of being anything like him. In that respect, maybe Frank, Sam, and I, along with countless others, owe Flint our gratitude for helping to make us all, even if unintentionally, better people. Flint would remain forever our most vivid model of what not to become as human beings.

The painful experiences we have, especially when we're young, can scar us, harden us, or give us a different kind of understanding and strength to face other things later on. Each one of us can probably think of a nemesis from his or her past, someone who seemed to enjoy making us miserable, but who could also make us appreciate others in our lives who had inspired us with their kindness or encouragement. The unhappy jobs we endured as stock boys in grocery stores serving thoughtless and rude customers, laborers in hot, uncomfortable factories, newspaper delivery boys, baby sitters for monster kids, or work at any other jobs we found to be all but unbearable, serve to give us the desire to do something else, something with creative satisfaction and meaning that goes right to the core of who we are and who we want to become. That need to look "elsewhere" stops perhaps when we discover our callings, that overwhelming and all consuming realization that in our work, we're doing what we were meant to do as our principal occupation or career in life. As a kid I had enjoyed playing school and pretending to be a teacher or principal, so the desire had always been there, but there are probably many who stumble upon their choices for work much later and by pure accident, but that doesn't diminish the power of finding one's own calling, whenever it happens.

Some kids know as early as middle school what their callings are. Others don't know until after high school, and still others never really know what they were meant to do, which is why I believe strongly in high schools having "career" days, where many choices are presented interestingly with large amounts of information and the chance for kids to ask questions. Options are needed so they can be matched with preferences and inclinations that may otherwise remain untapped or unrecognized, allowing some students to drift aimlessly toward conveyor belt jobs, where those people may or may not find their callings but stay just to get by. That isn't to say that kids are mere fodder for the work place, though it often seems that way, but finding what they like and do best seems vastly important to individuals and to society. Not everyone has to attend college, but the essential thing is to help kids know what's out there for them in the way of employment in which they can find some measure of significance, security, and pride.

Chapter 34 Time Capsules

One of the most wonderful parts of teaching was that I was able to keep in touch over the years with many of my former students, at first through snail-mail, then through e-mail and FaceBook.

In the early 1970's when I began to have classes of seniors at MHS, my students and I were talking one afternoon about how much change can occur in a person's life over a period of just ten years. I asked them to think back all those years to second grade and to try remembering whatever they could about that time in their lives and how life had changed since. Of course, they all sited huge differences between being eight years old and being eighteen, focusing much on the fact that they felt much more independent and aware in their late teens than they had felt ten years before.

Then I talked to them about some of the differences I saw between being eighteen and being my then current age of twenty-eight and assured them that the changes during those years were as vast as the changes from age eight to eighteen. I told them that aside from knowing that increased self-reliance was one of the central parts of adulthood, I still wasn't completely sure myself what it meant to be "grown up," but that I was still working on it and would probably continue working on it the rest of my life. We had already discussed at length Ralph Waldo Emerson's essay, "Self-Reliance" as an iconic piece of American literature, as well as Henry David Thoreau's book, WALDEN, and his essay, "On Civil Disobedience." The idea of worlds within ourselves as yet unexplored appealed to those students, and one line from WALDEN provided two class periods of intense discussion. "No man ever stood the lower in my estimation for having a patch in his clothes; yet I am sure that there is greater anxiety, commonly, to have fashionable, or at least clean and unpatched clothes, than to have a sound conscience."

I took a box of business envelopes to school, giving each senior one. Students wrote on the envelopes their own names and addresses with my name and the school as the return address. Then I asked students to think of the envelopes as time capsules. The next step was to write down titles of favorite songs, books, names of best friends, current personal conflicts believed to be "major," comments about their hopes and dreams with at least one specific goal central to what the next few years could bring, as well as at least one vivid memory from high school that each person believed he or she would keep forever.

The class was surprised when I said that I wouldn't be grading or even reading what they were putting into those "private" envelopes. Then I asked that the envelopes be sealed, and I provided cellophane tape to make sure the seals were secure. Finally, I asked that everyone write on the back of the envelope, "April, 1984," the date when I would be mailing the letters ten years down the road. So, 1974 was the first batch to be filed away for mailing in ten years. I told students that as there would be only one class per year for this experiment, that I would be happy to pay the postage when the time came for mailing.

The other request I made was that if and when the time capsules were received, that everyone take a few minutes in 1984 to write back to let me know how life was going and how those ten years had changed their lives. Naturally, the very real possibility of their parents moving away posed a risk we would have to take. More disturbing, if even more remote, was the chance that a student would pass away during those ten years, the macabre consequence being that parents would receive a letter in the handwriting of their deceased offspring. Students laughed when I brought up this unlikely contingency, but it remained a fearful possibility in my mind for many years, so that I always told the class to let their parents know about the letters arriving eventually.

An entire filing cabinet at home was devoted to storing those letters written by seniors over the years. The first set I mailed in April of 1984 at which time I was struck by the increase in postage, so that forever after I had students provide one stamp to help defray whatever increase in postage was bound to occur over the next decade. Because I retired in 2004, I still had sets of letters to mail each spring, and my last bunch will be mailed in April of 2014 to complete the thirty-year cycle of those time capsules. I'm still in contact with the school in order to receive responses that come each year.

That assignment was also a wonderful way to keep contacts open with former students, many of whom took time to send me updates, both happy and sad, about what those ten years had brought. Many responses included stories of divorce, photographs of children my students had, and comments about how much the unusual assignment had meant to them. Many found the letters' arrivals a total surprise after having forgotten all about them. A few letters came back, "address unknown," but most reached their destinations. Many also took the letters to their ten-year class reunions, but those time capsules kept open the doors of communication and gave me the grand chance to see, at least in some ways, how students' lives were turning out, and how productive their educations had been thus far.

One student in particular continued writing to me for many years. You may remember Jim Davis from an earlier chapter about my first year of teaching. He was the kid in my Basic English III and IV classes, who gave the famous karate demonstration speech, breaking a pine board at the conclusion of his speech. Jim became a trucker and until 1995 drove a big rig across the country, and during those years even wrote a book about his travels across America, called THE ROLLING ROAD, which was never published, but he lent me the manuscript, which reminded me of John Steinbeck's TRAVELS WITH CHARLIE. Then in the late 1990's Jim changed careers completely by opening his own Jewish funeral home in Palo Alto, California. He continued writing to me, sending me photos along the way of his second wife, his daughter, and finally his grandchildren. I still have the photo of him sitting on his big Harley Hog, smiling broadly with the caption, BORN TO BE WILD.

Those time capsule letters, begun in 1974, gave me the chance to create a continuum of communication over many years. Too often teachers see their students during part of all of the four years of high school before the conveyor belt stops after graduation, and nothing else is generally heard again, unless the kid's picture is seen at the post office, or on the ten o'clock evening news for a crime spree or winning a Nobel Prize. Those letters were a marvelous means to continue sharing news with many of the students who for me, would otherwise have disappeared completely, along with their many ventures and successes. I still exchange Christmas and Hanukkah cards with students I haven't seen since the 1970's. What other profession can create such a breadth of contacts over so many years, and the joy of knowing how well many of those people turned out, helping to confirm again and again what our work in the classroom really meant?

Chapter 35 Change

I had a pretend theory for my classes that the gray matter of our brains was actually coated with an organic substance very similar to the gray silicone inside an Etch-A Sketch, and if we moved too suddenly or awkwardly, things got "erased." The joke worked best on freshmen, some of whom seemed genuinely to believe the theory as fact. If I were explaining some new concept in grammar or literature, I might say, "OK, everybody, look right at me for a minute, listen, and don't move a muscle. I'm going to try writing something on your brains." Then I might have to rifle an accusation at someone, like, "Hey! You MOVED, Tommy! Do you remember what I just said, or did it get erased?" Sometimes humor works best, and the kids usually picked up on the fact that I was enjoying myself, and joined in. There are few people, who don't enjoy their own laughter.

The experience I had endured about Jasper Stickley's cheating in my class and all the ramifications that went with that terrible episode were all far behind me, and happily, nothing that depressing ever occurred again during the rest of my years at MHS. However, a personal bereavement that I and my colleagues suffered was the loss of our friend, Senora Mendoza, the teacher of Spanish with whom I had shared a fake but comical feud over the years. Our classrooms were across the hall from each other, our Spanish and French classes sometimes in competition to see if her students singing "La Cucaracha" could drown out my students' renditions of "La Marseillaise." Her classes under the new Spanish teacher would never again enjoy the vitality they had loved under Senora Mendoza. There would no longer be the aroma of Mexican food, the sounds of singing or laughter from her classroom, or the jokes we used to play on each other from time to time, the kids always happily in on our pranks.

Mrs. Mendoza's funeral was very well attended on a Saturday morning, and a beautiful sombrero and serape were placed over the closed casket that hid at last the emaciation that had been the result of the cancer.

The world was changing so much and so often, seemingly too fast, at least for me. The school invested in our first computers and a lab to house them, which changed the dynamic of composition forever. Teachers would be keeping attendance records and grades on computers in their classrooms. Bill Clinton was the President of our country, and it seemed suddenly that all of his brilliant and compassionate work was eclipsed stupidly by the Monica Lewinsky affair. There were more and more tattoos, body piercings, more students with spiked hair in brilliant colors not even found in nature, and clothing styles I didn't begin to understand, that included pants that didn't know if they were trying to be long shorts or short slacks, and clunky shoes that never appeared to fit the wearers. The angry and in-your-face music of Hip Hop and rap were everywhere, and almost frightened me into believing that I was growing old, even though I knew that trends all my life had come and gone, sometimes in the blink of an eye. The one thing that scared me and what I wanted most to avoid was the dreadful feeling of being left behind in the sense of not being able to keep up with what was going on. The truth was, however, that technology was racing ahead of most of us all at a pace with which no one could really keep up. The information highway had too many lanes for anyone to keep track of. I sometimes felt like someone driving a tiny bumper car competing with huge semi trucks.

Books remained anchors in my life so that whenever I thought the world was spinning too fast for me to feel a part of it, I could go back to a novel by Jane Austen or Charles Dickens to become grounded again by what was human through the flesh and blood stories in which I was always able to find something organic. Books I still go back to from time to time to feel in touch again with what is real and important are the ones by James Herriot, especially his ALL CREATURES GREAT AND SMALL and ALL THINGS BRIGHT AND BEAUTIFUL. The intelligence and sympathetic nature of those narratives always make me feel there's hope for a world that means well but is often speeding out of control. I think that most of my students shared my joy in those books, but I remained interested in the new books they were reading, good books that were not classics, but which said significant things about that teenage world inhabited by those in my classes. My students were the ones who got me hooked on the Harry Potter series.

In 1999 after my advanced French class had a fundraiser lasting several months through selling zillions of candy bars, having car washes, doing baby sitting jobs, and begging parents, grandparents, aunts and uncles to make up the differences, I took fifteen of those students and three parents to France, where we stayed mostly in Paris, but also visited the chateaux of the Loire Valley, villages in Brittany, the place in Rouen where Joan of Arc was burned at the stake, Normandy, where we stood on the esplanade overlooking Omaha Beach in the rain to remember D-Day, the battle that had changed the world forever. We also saw the American Museum and cemetery in Normandy, which had some of the kids in tears, after they watched a film about our soldiers being there, many buried in the beautiful spot which was named by the French government officially as American soil.

As it was April, the gardens at Versailles were in bloom, all the fountains dancing in the sunlight, the windows to the grand salons open to receive the fragrance of flowers on the gentle breezes, and the sounds of a baroque orchestra from one of the parterres playing music by Lully from the time of Louis XIV, the 17th Century king who had built the palace. It was an unforgettable morning and afternoon.

Back in Paris, only an hour away by train, I encountered the only problem of our entire trip. All the students on that trip were the best, most conscientious and most dependable from our school, but I had, for added safety, laid down some rules for any free time. First I insisted that students go out only in groups of three at least one of those students wearing a watch. Curfew was eleven o'clock every evening, and I would wait in the hotel lobby until everyone had checked in. One trio wanted to explore an area around the French Planet Hollywood, but at eleven-thirty that night they hadn't returned, and I was pacing the lobby almost ready to call a "gendarme" to report them missing. Just after midnight the three girls appeared as I was dozing off in one of the big stuffed chairs near the check-in desk. The girls had taken the wrong Metro line and ended up in Montmartre near the church of Sacre Coeur.

Before our trip I had received permission from all parents to take the group to the Vouvray vineyards, where each student was allowed to purchase up to six bottles of fine French wine without paying a tariff when we returned to the States. All those parents were delighted by their benefits from that part of our journey.

After 9/11 of 2001, I never again took a group to France. Nor did I have the desire to go back myself. The emotional climate of international travel and even domestic flights had changed overnight. The feelings of ease and safety in flying were gone forever, especially for parents who had become reluctant to allow their children to travel across our own country, let alone overseas. That sad ending to those wonderful years of travel had a powerful effect on my teaching French as well. Without the added incentive of that hope of seeing together the country whose language we were studying, something was lost in motivation. However, that didn't mean we could no longer enjoy speaking and writing French and appreciating the rich variety of food, music, literature, and history of France. The world had changed drastically and suddenly, so that we all had to adapt ourselves to resisting a savage and psychotic religious fanaticism the world had forgotten existed since the Spanish Inquisition.

Chapter 36 The Final Bell

A long time ago I stopped telling strangers at parties that I taught English, only because so many would simply clam up, as though afraid they might make a mistake in grammar and be sent to stand in a corner with their cocktails in hand. Also the word "teacher" conjures up so many conflicting images, because it is a word so rich in meaning, that revealing you're a teacher, without the chance to expound a bit on what that signifies, is a little like being thirty-nine years old but telling people you're thirty-something. Too much has to be left out, which is why I wrote this book to share what it meant to me working in a public school all those years.

My writing classes continued publication each spring of their anthologies of student writing and art work. Each book was between fifty and seventy pages of the best creative efforts of the school, which included submissions from freshmen through seniors. By 2004 the books had won three national awards from the National Council of Teachers of English. The EYEBROW JOYRIDE was the collection for 1995, WE COME IN PIECES for 1997, FALLING UP THE STAIRS (a Metaphor for Life) in 1998, and for 2003, the anthology was POETRY AND HEDONISTIC LIES. CLIFFDWELLERS was our final publication in 2004, the year I retired. All of those collections of student work over the years provided a product we were able to take with us and keep as something of which to remain proud. Some of my fondest memories of teaching involve working with students on those publications, and I still have tremendous respect for the love and effort that were put into each volume.

Faculty meetings continued to be anesthetizing experiences with most voices sounding to me like the adults in Charlie Brown cartoons. PTA meetings, open houses, parent conferences, Foreign Language Club field trips, speech and debate meets all over Indiana, Chess Club competitions at which we never even placed, curriculum and textbook committees, grading papers, planning lessons for five different classes per day, dealing with the occasional recalcitrant student, and with a few disagreeable and bitter colleagues, all managed to consume my life on a daily basis, even through the year when I taught summer school as well. It was a life that had meaning for me, because there was always a sense of purpose in working with kids. I had, by the fall of 2003, used over 1200 red pens, the remaining few, which would upon my retirement be buried in my garden during a celebratory ceremony, attended by friends, after which we cracked open a bottle of Veuve Clicquot Champagne, my garden roses becoming a bit redder that summer.

Those years of teaching were rich in the experience of being with people, and having taught over seven thousand students, I can now say that they were very wonderful years, years that kept me young in spirit. I was in room 242 most of those years, a room on the second floor facing the football field to the south. It was like a big terrarium, hot in spring and fall and frigid in winter...but a good portion of my heart will always remain there. My identity during all that time was that of a teacher. That was who I was when people asked what I did. I have stayed in contact with many of the students I had over all those years and had many whose parents I also had taught. The sense of community that afforded gave me a feeling of continuity and stability in a career in which most people don't last more than five years anymore.

I had excellent classes for the most part. The fall of 2003 I tackled a special English class of problem students. It was a freshman class with people who had behavioral problems, including past expulsions. This is the one story I must tell to help new teachers understand the meaning of all those years to me. It is a kind of microcosm that speaks of my love and respect for the profession. It will help to know me better and perhaps to understand better what teaching gives back.

It was a remarkable day in late September. Every day is remarkable in its own way, but I was touched by something unexpected during my last class of the day. Because it was Friday afternoon and the end of the school day with my most difficult class (the leather-jacket, juvenile delinquent crowd I have already mentioned), I was feeling sorry for myself, thinking as I watched them taking their Friday vocabulary test that I was not really reaching them as I had hoped to do. I saw my reflection in a big mirror that I used to keep tabs on everything that went on in the room even when my back was turned. My face looked sad. Though the rest of the day had been very successful and most enjoyable in my other classes, I was focusing once again on what I felt was a failure on my part to inspire everyone in the room and have them excited about what we were going to be doing after the test.

Then there was a knock on the door, and a messenger from the main office delivered a package to me that had just arrived. My students were distracted by the interruption (always an arduous task to get them back on track after ANY distraction, even a sneeze). One bold kid in the front row (the one who was proud that his brother was in prison for armed robbery) asked who it was from and what it was.

I read the return address and said that the package was from a former Morton student, Jim Davis, from many years ago (thirty-four to be exact). One kid joked that it might be a bomb, but I replied that I was going to open it anyway and that we would all go up together...like bottle rockets.

Their curiosity was aroused by now, and excuses for distraction aside, they were genuinely interested to know the contents. I opened the box to find a five-page letter from that former student , who was a trucker for twenty-five years before opening his own mortuary in California. He had been in a "problem" class just like the one I was teaching that hour...a "basic skills" English class. We corresponded over all those intervening years, and he continued to send me news about his life, including, at last, pictures of his grand children.

He worked for several months after 9/11 at Ground Zero clearing debris and corpses. He worked with the New York city Fire Department and Police Department as head coroner. In the box was the cap he wore during his work there. It was covered with dirt and badges for his valor. It was the thing of which he was most proud. The letter said that I had always been his favorite teacher and that he still thought of the ways I had inspired him to be his best even though he was now fifty-one years old. He wanted me to have the cap, because he was proud of it, and I was his hero in a time when the world was calling him a hero.

My eyes filled up as I looked at it and explained to the class what it was. They were absolutely silent (perhaps the first time they had ever seen a teacher cry). The bell rang and they left quietly (as they had never done before). Maybe they too were touched by what had occurred. I don't know. It may be that they were simply shocked by my reaction. It didn't matter. I had not been so moved in a long time by a gesture like that gift. It came at just the right time to let me know that teaching had indeed made a difference and that there were influences that continued long after students were gone. I felt quite blessed.

Jim had heart surgery two weeks after he sent me the cap and died October 23, 2003. I'll include the final letter I sent to him before his death. I retired the following spring.

September 19, 2003

Dear Jim,

Your package arrived today during my most difficult class (the leather- jacketed delinquent set). They all have learning disabilities and I often feel that I am not reaching them and that my work is of no use. Just keeping order in the class is a constant and draining job. So much for my whining.

One student in the front row asked what the package was and how had sent it. When I answered that it had come from a former student, someone said, "Look out! It might be a bomb." I replied that I was going to open it anyway and that we would all go up together like bottle rockets. I read only part of your letter before my eyes filled up. When I came to the cap, I lost my composure and sobbed. The students were absolutely silent. They saw how very moved I was and I believe they understood what I was feeling. I don't think I have ever been so proud or touched by any other gift in my whole life as I was that cap and that letter. It suddenly made my whole career make sense. It helped me to know that what I do is not in vain and that positive influences continue even after my students have moved on to other things and other places.

I can't tell you, Jim, how much it meant to me to receive what you sent. I shared it with some people in the main office downstairs before I left school today, and they cried too. What a beautiful gesture you made!

Please know that you will be in my thoughts and prayers. I will want to know how the surgery went and that everything is going well for you again. You are an extraordinary man of great courage and gallantry. In spiritual terms there is nothing wrong with your heart. It is the best and biggest one I know.

Of all the students I have taught over the past thirty-five years, you will remain the one for whom I keep the fondest regard. That cap will be on my bookshelf always to remind me of the valor and compassion you have shown your fellow-beings. You have taught me at least as much as I have taught you.

Your friend,

John Bolinger

Wherever I am, I still think often of Morton High School, a building I entered for the first time in my early twenties, a place that for me will always echo the voices of thousands of students, who have passed through its halls, the sounds of chalk on blackboards, the turning of millions of pages in books, the bounce of basketballs on the gym floor, the roar of crowds cheering at touchdowns on the football field, the crack of the ball and bat, the music of choirs, orchestras, and bands slightly out of tune, a place where so many young people became men and women.

Clusters of powerful recollections flooded my mind that afternoon of June 9, 2004 as I finished putting final grades on scan sheets. For lunch my friend Logan Clark had taken me to a favorite Chinese restaurant, where we also polished off a large pitcher of Mai Tai before going back to school, where I said my goodbyes to custodians, office staff, and some teachers, who were still grading papers and putting final grades on the scan sheets. Then I gathered up my electric box fan, and old Zenith mahogany radio from 1955.

At the door to my classroom, I turned to look once more at where I had taught for so many years, a room uncharacteristically silent that afternoon, as I turned out the lights and closed the door for the last time. I went down the same stairway I had climbed and descended so many thousands of times. The parking lot was almost empty, as I loaded my car trunk. Driving from the lot, I saw the school building grow smaller in my rear-view mirror, a shrinking image that became almost a mirage as I sped off into the warmth of approaching summer. It was over.

The following autumn, I would continue to wave at the school bus passing my house as I raked leaves. The journey Bel Kaufman had told me about thirty-five years before had certainly provided more than I could ever have imagined. She was right about that. And now, if I were young again with the energy I once had, I would happily begin that journey again.